When a Relationship Ends

When a Relationship Ends

Surviving the Emotional
Roller-Coaster of Separation

Lisa O'Hara

ORPEN PRESS

Published by Orpen Press
Lonsdale House
Avoca Avenue
Blackrock
Co. Dublin
Ireland

e-mail: info@orpenpress.com
www.orpenpress.com

ISBN: 978-1-871305-23-4

Printed in Ireland by Colorman Ltd.

Acknowledgements

This book has been written with the help and encouragement of many people and I deeply appreciate their unwavering generosity.

First, I am grateful to my employers, Relationships Ireland, for the use of their library and resources. Without the encouragement of Chief Executives Kevin Smyth and Brendan Madden this book would not have been possible. I am aware of how busy counselling always is, but they believed it was important for me to take time to write the book in order to provide help to as many people as possible who are going through difficult times in their relationships, regardless of whether they are together or separated.

Thank you also to the many counsellors in Relationships Ireland and Teen Between who gave me their time when I was trying to figure out how to make counselling theory understandable. They provided useful suggestions that really matter to people who are separating and to people who are involved in the separating person or their family's lives. Special thanks to Eithne Bacuzzi, Gerry Cullen, Yvonne Jacobson, Pauline Keane, Kathleen Lambert, Jerry MacDonough, Francesca McGuinn, Chris McNally, Christine May, Tony Moore, Jacinta O'Herlihy, Anne Mathews and Bernadette Ryan.

I am grateful to experts outside the counselling field who also deal professionally in the area of separation and divorce in Ireland, namely Rita Hurson, Clara Clark, Caroline Gore-Grimes and Claire Kearney. They gave me a more comprehensive perspective on issues that face people during separation and divorce.

I am grateful for the support and encouragement of my editor, Elizabeth Brennan, who always made herself available; her patience with me led me to believe that writing this was possible and within my capability.

It was always much easier to write when I went to the West of Ireland and I deeply appreciate the generosity of David, Mary-Jo, Aoife and Antóin Stanton, who gave me the run of their home in Kerry whenever I needed it. I am also grateful to Seán and Oonagh Cooke for their hospitality during the more intensive periods of writing and to Pat Stanton as well as Pat, Kathleen, Jackie and Siobhán Murphy who kept me company during the breaks. Thanks, too, to Glynis Good who helped me to focus on the difficult chapter on co-parenting and invited me to her home in Clifden, where we could start the work away from any distractions.

I am also indebted to my friends who didn't mind when I was out of contact for long stretches when writing. Thanks to Colin Blake, Aoife Coffey, James Hancock, Yann Lefebvre and Donna Sunario who took time to read parts of the book. Also, I am grateful to Ultan Mulligan, and Claire and Garry Cleary, whose generosity allowed me to stay at the keyboard during a difficult family illness.

I am grateful to my family for knowing that I could do this. We have laughed and cried over many losses in our lives. We have survived and grown both as individuals and together, and have fortunately remained close. I am incredibly proud to belong with you.

And finally, to all those people who have taken the risk of giving me permission to tell their stories. This book is a composite of what the end of relationships is really about. Courage cannot exist without fear. In truth, I could never do your bravery justice. Thank you.

Contents

Introduction

Ireland is a country well known for its grieving rituals when there is bereavement through death. We mourn the dead person; we talk about them and what they meant to us. Generally speaking, we prefer to idealise the deceased, perhaps as a way of minimising our own grief and to give dignity to the person who has died. We are taken care of by others as we prepare for the funeral, and are rarely left alone during that time.

There is even a language that we use to convey our sympathy – 'I'm sorry for your loss' or 'my deepest sympathy' – and the grieving person responds to the sympathetic words by nodding their head or saying 'thank you' in acknowledgement. We can cry openly and lament publicly for our departed loved one, even if we didn't get on so well with them when they were alive. There is usually a lot of support and care available to us during this mourning period. Being largely a Catholic country, a month after the funeral we remember the person who has died with the month's mind.

It is widely accepted that this is a sad time for surviving loved ones, whether the death came suddenly or was anticipated, and that those in mourning will need time to get over such a loss. Death is final. The loved one is gone. Nothing can be done to change that.

Separation, on the other hand, could be described as the 'living death'. The difference between death through bereavement and the death of a relationship is that your partner is still alive, which can make it a more complex loss from which to recover. There is no corpse to mourn, and there is no definite date (in most cases anyway) of separation – is it when the news was broken, when a couple physically separate or when the separation papers are signed? Or does separation happen long before that, when one or both partners realised that they were no longer in love? Rather than idealise or think well of our ex-partner, it is instead usual to criticise or blame the ex-partner, even if you still have feelings for them.

Separation from your partner is a major life crisis and ranks highly in terms of stress, along with other big changes such as death, changing jobs, getting married and health issues. Even though separation and divorce have been legalised for well over a decade, people still remain awkward around the issue. It's hard to know what to say. Unlike death, there is no set language that can convey to the separating person your acknowledgement and sympathy about what has happened.

And what about the separating or separated person? How do they respond? What do they say to others, even if they are ready to speak, without going into too much detail? Will others want to know more than you, as the separated person, are ready to share or will you overwhelm them with too much information? Separation can be a traumatic time when you feel defenceless and vulnerable. As a result, personal boundaries can disappear or become so reinforced (to protect yourself) that you allow no one in and you become isolated from the rest of the world.

It is natural for people to be curious about why couples break up. If the separated/separating person decides to go into any explanation, they might often get to hear about the enquiring friend's relationship woes, which may only be an attempt to empathise with the person who is grieving, but can be irritating and upsetting. Moreover, how can you talk about your separation with dignity and remain composed? When a person dies, everyone accepts it as normal if you become emotional. If neither you nor the person you are talking to have ever experienced separation before, it can be very uncomfortable. What is probably the worst experience is when separation is *ignored* altogether, when no one says anything, as if nothing at all happened. Without acknowledgement and understanding of the necessary grieving journey that accompanies such a huge life change, separation can become more complicated than it needs to be.

What is common to both death and separation, however, is a deep mourning process or journey that has no time limit. A common myth is that getting over a loss this significant usually takes 'two falls of the seasons' or, in other words, two years. The reality is that it takes as long as it takes! The intensity and length of mourning can be proportionate to the importance and meaning that the relationship had for each person. In addition to this, the practicalities of physically separating, especially when the couple cannot finalise their own separation agreement together, can prolong a separation, often for years. Some people will never seem to mourn – perhaps they have done their grieving before the relationship ended or maybe they ensure they go from relationship to relationship in order to avoid feeling any pain at all.

A well-known adage is not to make any major life decisions in the first six months to a year following the death of a loved one. This can also apply to the period following separation, because people are uncertain about how to proceed and leave matters on an informal footing until the dust has settled. In any event, if they can afford to physically separate and leave everything else as it is, they may see no need for a formal separation agreement – unless, for whatever reason, one or both feel that it's time to sort out their affairs. For others, things have to be sorted more immediately due to the financial pressure of having to live in two separate homes and they do not have the luxury of time. Unfortunately, decisions made during an emotional time can be ill-considered and may be regretted later.

Grieving over the loss of an important relationship is like the ebb and flow of the tide, it goes in and it goes out, it becomes intense and then it eases. But the grief is always there. Do we ever really get over this loss or is it better to expect that we will manage it in a manner whereby it can be woven into the tapestry of our lives, as the power of our grief lessens with time?

The purpose of this book is to give you a better understanding of your internal world as you go through separation. Just like love, separation has many stages or phases. It is not an event. It does not happen on one day and then it's done. For those who are newly separated, it is best to be aware that separation is a marathon rather than a sprint. It is true that along the way we can develop a resilience that keeps us going, even if we have to stop and take a breather for a while. People who have gone through separation report that they discover a personal strength they weren't aware they were capable of. It can be hard to believe this, especially in the early stages when you're so raw and confused a lot of the time, but, I promise you, it does happen and you will get past where you are now. Grieving is important and healthy, even if, paradoxically, it is painful. The main emotions associated with grief, regardless of which stage of the separation journey you are at, are highlighted throughout this book.

The book also touches on gender differences that can cause problems, not only when you are actively in a relationship, but also at the separation stage. It may help you to understand why it seems natural for you to behave in a certain way, while your ex-partner seems to behave quite differently, thus heightening your confusion, anger and anxiety.

Above all, I wish for this book to give the reader hope – hope that, although separation may feel like the worst thing in the world, this seemingly unending period will pass. Your life will begin again when you are ready. Even though it may feel like there's no end to the dark days, especially at the early stages, and life truly feels hopeless, you will get the odd day when you smile and even find yourself laughing. As times goes on, you will get more of those good days. You will also get bad days, when you feel nothing has really changed. But, actually, it has. When you experience one good day, it means you are starting to recover. You will have more of those good days again.

New opportunities will come and you will get to make decisions for yourself that may not have been possible when you were still part of a couple. It is common for people who have gone through the separation journey to become more interested in themselves, not in a selfish way, but more out of curiosity as to the aspects of themselves that define them as a person and to identify where there is scope for personal development. The book provides some useful ideas to help you get started.

The book may also provide some clues for others who are an integral part of the separating/separated person's life to help them get a better grasp of what the separation journey entails. It aims to normalise the seemingly abnormal. People who have close relationships with the separated person are often at a loss to know what to do to help, not realising just how beneficial their support and encouragement really is. Yet, they cannot rescue or fix what has happened. They may want take the pain away but that's not possible either. It is their love and regard for the separated person that keeps them connected to them, while the grieving person is proceeding on their journey. A family member or a friend may also be grieving over the loss of that relationship, especially if there are children involved or they liked their friend or family member's ex-partner. They may feel they have to choose sides and it becomes confusing for everyone. Ergo, separation has a ripple effect and many lives are touched. If the couple never married but lived their lives as if they were, the ending of their relationship will have a similar effect. As long as a relationship involved a personal commitment on the part of the couple, the loss of that relationship will have had a deep and serious meaning for them both.

Finally, I wish you the very best. This is a tough journey – only those who have been through it will really understand. It stands alone as a unique experience. You stand alone as well, and there are times when you might feel incredibly isolated from the outside world, a world where you are not really understood. Because separation and divorce are relatively new in this country, it is only in the last few years that groups of people who have had this experience have started coming together in an effort to support each other and find some comfort and understanding of what has happened. One of the best things about the internet is that it has made the world a smaller place and we have access to information that can also help. I encourage you to arm yourself as best you can with whatever you need to get over the difficult times, whether it is information, supportive friends or family, or professional help, such as counselling.

Chapter 1

Falling in Love and Why Break-Ups Happen

Many people who are going through separation will wonder how they got to this point. Where did it all go wrong? Why did their relationship not go the distance and what was particular about the bond they had with their ex-partner that meant their relationship would come to an end one day, while other couples stayed together? Following separation, searching for answers to these questions can become a preoccupying pastime for many, as they seek to find meaning in such a devastating experience. This chapter explores some of these questions and may help you discover some of the not-so-helpful patterns that contribute to relationship conflict and, for some, a subsequent break-up.

Have you ever wondered why we fall in love with one person and not another; why we fall in love with someone and have an overwhelming feeling of excitement when we think about them, and long for them when we're apart?

Some people would describe love as instant and for others it's a slow burner. For all, though, love is a connection with someone that defies words and has an almost ethereal quality.

Typically, when we are attracted to someone and then that attraction starts to grow, it gives us a body sensation, like an electrical charge, and this is what we call chemistry. It is the moment when possibly we start to hope that we have met 'the one', our true love, our soul mate. This is also the time when we unconsciously ask our partner to make all our wishes come true for the 'perfect' relationship. An easy way to describe this is to imagine we each have a 'chip', similar to that found on a mobile phone SIM card, and that chip contains all the information about our wishes, dreams and expectations for love. When we fall in love, we effectively offer this chip to our partner in the hope that they will take it from us and operate from that chip *only*. What we don't anticipate is that they too have a chip that *they* offer us that may have a different interpretation of longings and needs for the perfect relationship.

All of this goes on silently, even unconsciously, in the early stages of a relationship. We don't even know each other well yet. We are attracted to the other person's looks, the things they say, a quality they might have or a way they behave that makes us believe that this person will take on the responsibility of operating from our chip. Physiologically, we may be experiencing that tingling feeling or butterflies in our tummy. This is a time of yearning (tinged with anxiety), yet it is exciting too.

In the initial stages of falling in love, we are seeking to develop a strong bond with our partner. In order to do that, we usually try to spend as much time as possible with each other, if not physically then by other modes of staying connected – texting, phone, email, Twitter, etc. When we're apart, we become aware that we are missing the other person and we look forward to being together again. This period, the initial attraction stage, may be very intense. It is also a time for sharing our hopes and dreams, and finding the things that we have in common. We are, generally speaking, on our best behaviour. We want to work from our partner's chip and they from ours. In those first heady months, we may even experience a little blip or two when our new partner behaves in a way that we are not happy with, but we cover it over or ignore it to keep any feelings of dissatisfaction or unhappiness to a minimum – we like our new relationship overall and accept that no one's perfect.

In those first halcyon days or months of a relationship, we make a good effort to try to please the other person in order to keep them happy and thus keep the relationship secure and intact. It is still fragile and we will do what we can to protect it, if we believe it might have a future. In order to progress the relationship and strengthen the bond, we do or say things that generate good feelings when we are together, and we feel the pain of missing that person when we are apart. We find ourselves in a dream-like state and every day has an almost magical quality. We are indeed falling in love.

Where Does Our Need for Love Come From?

Many theorists would say that we are trying to re-create that first love bond, the symbiotic relationship between mother and child. Before he or she is born, a child's needs are met through an umbilical cord in the womb. Following birth, the mother continues to see to those needs, soothing the child's pain, covering her baby when he or she is cold, and feeding him or her when they are hungry, essentially protecting her child's life. Gomez (1998, p. 86) summarises the mother–child bond through the eyes of psychoanalyst Donald W. Winnicott as one where 'the infant becomes a personal self through the protective care of the "good-enough mother".' She may be obsessed with her new-born baby and rarely leave him; ' .... [S]he fosters an illusion of oneness with her baby which makes him feel secure and even omnipotent.'

If this is the case, one could ask whether we are reasonable in our quest to recreate that seemingly perfect love that is bestowed without us even having to say what we want? Do we believe our partner will just intuitively understand what we need and provide it, regardless of their own needs? After all, we are supposed to come first in a love relationship! As adults, we accept that we can't always get our own way and, yet, we are still disappointed or hurt when our partner says 'no'. It can feel like rejection or that they don't care. The reality is our partner will let us down and reject us from time to time and sometimes for long periods in the relationship, but our bodies still hold the memory of those initial infant stages, when our mother didn't come the moment we cried, when we had to wait for her – *when she didn't put us first*. Even in that first year of life, we had to learn to deal with disappointment and disillusionment, and being a separate individual from her.

Later in our development, at around the age of one, we looked for our mother's encouragement and approval when we made progress in terms of independence – crawling, walking, etc. When we took our first steps, was our mother there to watch us and encourage us on, helping us to stand straight and stay confident enough to keep going? Or was she critical or panicky because she was afraid we would hurt ourselves and thereby causing us to feel shame or embarrassment at our efforts? Or did she even notice us at all when we looked to her for reassurance and encouragement?

We don't remember things like this consciously, but, as mentioned earlier, our bodies still hold the memory of the distress we felt when our needs went unmet. Over the course of our lives, we learn how to cope with this distress and, depending on how we do that, we react accordingly, i.e. we become angry, withdrawn or clingy, or we can rationalise that if we ignore the fact we won't have to deal with the hurt.

In addition to our relationship with our mother, our observations of our parents' relationship in childhood can have a major effect on our adult relationships. One of the pioneers of family therapy, Virginia Satir, believes that parents often dictate the template of their children's sexual and romantic lives: 'As children growing up in a family, we witness the couple relationship of our parents. What we observe exerts a powerful influence. Most people will choose the familiar, even though uncomfortable, over the unfamiliar, because of that power' (1989, p. 144).

This may help explain, theoretically anyway, why people are attracted to a partner who reminds them of one of their parents and why it can feel like they have a relationship similar to their parents'. This is neither a good thing nor a bad thing;

it is just what is familiar. There may have been some aspects of your parents' relationship you liked and wanted to emulate and some you didn't.

As we move into adolescence, we see the beginnings of adult love, where two individuals meet each other and are attracted to each other, both looking to have their emotional and sexual needs met. It is an intense time as these young couples are full of passion for each other. According to Viorst, '[M]any of us are done with adolescence before we are done with adolescent love' (2002, p. 185).

Our developmental history shapes what we expect from a relationship and we hold this on our chip. Some of those expectations may be entirely unconscious and we may be searching for a person with whom we can complete the 'unfinished business of childhood' (Viorst 2002, p. 192). For example, if we had a parent who wasn't available to us for whatever reason, we might hope now to have a relationship where our partner will give us the attention that we missed out on as a child. Or if we had an overprotective parent, we might be attracted to someone who is like that but with whom we can negotiate a more healthy distance in our adult relationship.

So, what happens when we finally meet someone who we believe fits us perfectly? Think about the pressure on that relationship and the responsibility we give to the other person never to let us down, frustrate us or fail us in any way; and the responsibility we take upon ourselves that we will be able to meet the other person's every need as they demand it, and that we will never hurt them or make them angry or upset. This has an unreal element, an almost fantasy-like feel to it. But it is what falling in love is all about, and people who quickly pull themselves back from unrealistic expectations will adjust better to being in a relationship. If you do this, you learn to accept the other for *who they are*, rather than thinking about them in terms of *what they can do to fulfil your needs*.

Marriage or a significant relationship, we hope, will fulfil our emotional and romantic dreams and yet will need to sustain itself through the more ordinary and mundane routines of life. Falling in love means that on some level we may put our partner on a pedestal as we discover things we really like and admire about them. It's hard not to place them there when we find ourselves falling deeply in love. Yet to keep them there and not see them as fallible human beings, the same as ourselves, means that the relationship takes on an unbalanced quality whereby the 'adorer' is always looking up and the 'adored' is looking down. Neither will feel equal (or on a par) with the other. The goal of a healthy relationship is being able to see the good qualities in ourselves that are worthy of love, as well as seeing the lovable qualities in our partner, a relationship where both can tolerate and understand each other's shortcomings. One partner's perception of the other's shortcomings may be more rooted in their own unrealistic expectations or fantasy: the idea of what you want your partner to be rather than who they really are.

Coming to Terms with Being Different

In their book, *Therapy with Couples*, gender experts Crowe and Ridley say:

> A man may usually hope for a trusting relationship within which his need to express himself physically and sexually can be contained. Women, on the other hand, may look for a relationship where the mutual expression of shared feeling is a priority. Where gender differences occur and are neither recognised nor respected they may be experienced as irritations or as deliberate acts to avoid, punish, dominate or control the relationship. (Crowe and Ridley 2000, p. 19)

It would make sense, therefore, that, within a relationship, when each partner fails to acknowledge and appreciate the other's needs sooner or later they begin to notice struggles emerging between them. We look to our partner to change (or

12

come around to our way of thinking), so we no longer feel the tension of being that separate from or different to them. If you take a moment to think about it, what a couple agrees on or feels the same about will not usually cause distress. Indeed, it is part of the glue that keeps a relationship strong. That's why it's important, before you commit yourself to a relationship, to explore how much glue you have holding you together. Differences between people cause the tension within relationships. In healthy relationships, where there is enough glue, couples will manage to integrate their differences and, where there is respectful regard for each other, this will be done without too much disturbance to the relationship.

As we begin to experience this degree of separation from our partner, we may subsequently yearn for the closeness once more. Yet, we retain a slight wariness of them, as we realise that they are not who we thought they were. And so we make up with them or they make up with us, and we once again return to the warm love cocoon. Although the desire will naturally be to negotiate our relationship differences, sometimes, depending on the personalities involved, things can blow up into an argument or a less verbal affair where doors are slammed and silence reigns for a while. But there will also be occasions when we might suppress entirely our hostile and hurt feelings in favour of being friends and lovers once again. In this case, we don't want to fall out with our partner and, in order to avoid conflict, we let them have their way and to do what they want. The feelings that are unexpressed or not dealt with are packed away and when the next 'pinch' comes (because it inevitably will), we are once again faced with the choice of resolving the present conflict or ignoring it. It shouldn't be surprising, therefore, that if a couple do not make peace with their differences they are more likely to find those feelings of love and goodwill wearing thin and other more negative feelings taking their place. Central to many couples' struggles is the challenge to agree on the amount of closeness (intimacy) and distance (separateness) their relationship needs, be it sexual, emotional, physical or operational (day-to-day living), in order for them both to be satisfied.

John (46) and Mary (42) have been married for nineteen years. Like many couples, they had their first child just after their first anniversary, and she was closely followed at two-year intervals by three more. With four children, their home was a busy one and it seemed to make sense that Mary would take time off work and bring up the children until they were school-going age. She would often say to John in those early years that she needed a bit of time away from the humdrum routine but, because he was busy trying to provide for everyone at home, he dismissed her requests that they go away for a night or weekend together without the children. Finally, she stopped saying anything about it. In fact, she stopped complaining at all, believing it would fall on deaf ears, so what was the point?

When their youngest child started his teenage years and was sent off to boarding school, Mary told John she wanted to separate. He was taken totally by surprise because he thought everything was going well. Although their sex life had dwindled over the years, they never argued about anything. Sadly, for Mary, all those unhappy feelings had gone to ground but had not disappeared. Instead, they had rotted away inside her, taking with it any love she had for him. She wanted a relationship where she could be heard and acknowledged, and not have her feelings trivialised as if they meant nothing. Things had gone a 'pinch' too far for her and she wanted out.

In this particular case, Mary, as a mother, may have been looking for more physical and non-verbal closeness, a need that may have been met if John had been around more. Perhaps John might have been seeking a resumption of the sexual closeness that is often put on the back burner when couples become parents and the needs of a child are so consuming.

Communication and Gender

Another source of difference in a relationship can be gender based. Communication of needs ranks as one of the highest problematic factors in relationships. A man wants to please his woman and make her happy. He wants her to trust him but when she gives him unasked for advice (even though she's only trying to help him) he may pick up the message that she thinks he doesn't know what he's doing. When he does not feel appreciated or trusted by her, he becomes de-motivated and withdraws his attention, love and passion. According to relationship expert John Gray, a man is usually happiest in a relationship when his woman is fulfilled. His efforts to please her and her trust in him 'makes him feel masculine, his body is filled with the fire of desire to get close, and he becomes purposeful. He feels inspired to be better, and he is motivated to fulfil her needs' (1999, p. 72). He wants to feel like he is adding to her life rather than being a burden to her. Ergo, he is very sensitive to any perceived criticism from her as this can make him feel like he's failing her somehow. He goes on to say: 'in order to keep a man attracted to her, a woman does not need to compete with the fantasy of women in the media and strive to create a perfect body. Instead, she needs to work toward communicating positive and nonrejecting messages ...' (p. 102). She doesn't have to keep her feelings from him; in fact, quite the opposite. Men like to know how a woman is feeling, but it's the manner in which she delivers it that counts. If she's able to say something like, 'I am feeling lonely without you. I miss you and know that you're busy at the moment. I just wanted you to know that' she has given *expression* to her feelings, while acknowledging her partner's situation as well. The opposite of this is when she *reacts* to her feelings and blames him for her distress: 'Why are you never home? I'm always on my own. You seem to be off enjoying yourself and leaving me with the boring stuff.' Can you see the difference? She is saying the same thing, but rather than owning her feelings, she is placing responsibility for them onto him.

A male is far more likely to respond positively to the first scenario because it's giving him a chance, without overwhelming him, to stay close to his partner and help her out. Men respond much more positively to a woman who is in control and assertively states her needs, rather than a woman who takes a passive aggressive approach. Passive aggressiveness plays out when people don't express themselves directly, but rather try to hint or manipulate others so that they get their needs met. Unfortunately, others usually will feel guilt or resentment as a result, and the last thing they'll want to do is respond to the need.

Aggressive (competitive) women are usually seen by men as one of their own, someone to spar with and debate with, but this really doesn't bring out the best in him romantically. His guard will be up constantly, so when she needs the softer, romantic side of him, he really doesn't know what to do, except to treat her like he would treat a man, which is to compete and debate. Nowadays, with more equal opportunities, women are expected to be as strong and as successful as men in the workplace. They may earn similar incomes and work the same hours, but when they finally get home they are faced with sharing the tasks of home life, including taking care of children. If their parents had the more traditional roles of provider and homemaker/nurturer, it can be difficult for them to negotiate who does what in a modern relationship, where these two quite different roles have now become blended.

It's little wonder that it becomes confusing for a man when his role of taking care of his partner is being blocked, as she assumes a more independent role from him. Sadly, even simple gestures like opening and closing doors for women, and being allowed to pay for dinner or drinks, are being lost. He is being deprived of the opportunity to do things for her without her having to ask so she knows she is cherished and that he is watching out for her and considering her needs. Even the most self-contained, independent women will soften towards a man when he extends himself like this.

Many women like to talk to share information, to think out loud, to express their feelings in order to create intimacy and closeness. They feel better because they have done so (Gray 1993). When a man doesn't recognise that his partner is expressing her needs as a woman, he might treat her as he would a fellow male, leaving her space and time to herself to sort out her problem, like he might need if he was upset. If he does this, she will feel he is ignoring or dismissing her. When a man doesn't listen or pay attention to his partner and her feelings, or when she is reluctant to share her feelings, her happiness with him will deteriorate and she loses her belief that her relationship is a good one (Gray 1993).

Different Types of Relationships

I've noticed over years of working with couples that there are a number of common types or styles of relationship. In my experience, couples usually adopt characteristics of one or more types. Some of the more common types of relationship incorporate characteristics of the following:

Validating

This is a 'we' relationship; a relationship that is described in 'we' rather than 'I' terms. Such a couple are polite to each other, give each other space and might use humour with each other in order to get their point across. They can negotiate and compromise and are generally good friends to each other. One of the qualities that may be missing from the relationship, however, is passion.

Volatile

This kind of relationship is full of passion. Strong beliefs are held and expressed by both partners. They may compete with each other and may be vulnerable to misunderstandings. There may be a lot of teasing, but the danger of this is that it can get out of hand during a period of instability. However, they can express more uncomfortable feelings to each other and move on.

Avoidant

This is a calm and an easygoing relationship. Such a couple are likely to have a strong sense of shared values. Their disagreements are seen as superficial rather than major setbacks. However, they may be leading parallel lives and the relationship itself may not be very passionate.

As you can see, there are benefits and downsides to each style. No type is ideal (we are, after all, human). When a relationship runs into difficulty, we tend to see our partner as the one who is 'the problem' rather than seeing that it is our own reaction to what they're doing and how it affects us that helps or hinders us in moving past any tension that is evident. So, for example, if you believe you always have to be the one who has to plan and book things, while your partner leaves you to it, you may become irritated and start thinking your partner has the easy end of the bargain. Although it could well be that your partner is lazy, deeper exploration may uncover their fear of being criticised by you if they do try to take over, thereby making them less likely to try it. Or they would rather avoid an argument because they find it upsetting or don't want to upset you. They want to keep the peace and the only way they see to do this is to let you have your way. If you want to share tasks, you will have to accept and trust your partner's ability to complete them successfully, in their own way and in their own time.

Another point to consider is that when we feel like we're left to do everything, we can fail to appreciate that our partner may well feel they are doing their fair share but in another area. For example, one person takes care of the bulk of the housework while the other becomes the primary breadwinner. Failure to appreciate the other person's effort means that resentment is more likely to surface in the long term, whether or not it is expressed.

Falling Out of Love

It doesn't take an expert to read the signals that a relationship might be heading for trouble. It can start with complaints (perhaps masked by humour) in front of friends or family. Maybe you find yourself sighing when once again you feel disappointed, angry, frustrated or just simply sad that your partner has let you down. Or maybe you've heard the same story from your partner a million times over and find yourself becoming either bored or irritated by it. Leading research scientist on marriage and family John Gottman conducted studies over many years and has found that the presence of what he calls 'The Four Horsemen of the Apocalypse' largely determines whether a relationship will succeed or fail. These four factors are *criticism* (different to a complaint, the purpose of which is to address something the person has done rather than be a global attack on their character), *contempt* (sneering, eye-rolling, sarcasm, name-calling and so on – it conveys disgust), *defensiveness* (a form of saying to your partner that they are the problem, not you) and *stonewalling* (withdrawing or ignoring the other). Although they are all harmful to the couple's love, Gottman believes that contempt is the most damaging as it is an unmistakable expression of 'long-simmering negative thoughts about the partner' (1999, p. 31).

Problems in relationships can build a cycle of negativity that can go on for years, a gradual eroding of what once was. There are times, however, when love can disappear quickly when some unforgivable act is committed and recovery can seem impossible. And so, the relationship ends.

We can sit with the unsettling realisation of not being in love with our partner anymore for quite some time without doing anything. Maybe we hope that this 'out of love' feeling will pass (and sometimes it does) or else the feeling of urgency eventually hits us and we feel we have no other choice but to leave the relationship. According to Judith Viorst:

> many marriages fail in mid-life because someone feels a 'do or die' urgency ... thus, if we find that our marriage meets too few of our expectations, or if it is good enough and we want great, or if – although we recognise that marriage means ambivalence – we are feeling far less love than hate, we may start raising the question of why not seek a new relationship before we get too faded and juiceless and scared? (2002, p. 276)

It is inevitable that long-term relationships will change over time because life itself is constantly changing and we weather those changes – ageing, childbearing, childrearing, death, illness, job changes, house moves, etc. Some couples endure several changes (each bringing its own losses and risks) and do not have a chance to recover from one before they embark on the next challenge. This is when relationships become particularly vulnerable.

Our experiences continually shape us and our attitudes. Our needs change and what was once vital to us may no longer have the same importance. Some couples find that there is no one thing that causes them to grow apart. Rather, it is the gradual growth of mutual indifference over the years. Some couples become so focused on the very important role of providing for and nurturing their children that each partner forgets that they were once in love with the other.

Relationships ending can be down to perceived selfishness on the part of one person, a sense of the relationship being unequal somehow or a developing intolerance of each other. There might be a basic incompatibility problem, which can happen when people become a couple too quickly without being able to assess whether they really are a good fit for each other in terms of their basic values and attitudes, interests, background, development and needs. Perhaps there was a lack of sufficient honesty and trust in a relationship, or there was an act of infidelity, or an inability to be able to communicate effectively so that each could be heard and understood by the other.

Regardless of how a relationship ends, it is quite common to hear people say things like, 'What did I ever see in him in the first place?' or 'How could I have been so stupid to have put up with it for so long?' or even 'I love her but I'm not in love with her.'

Once we have come to the point where we question whether we want to continue in the relationship, even if we haven't spoken a word, our partner may be sensitive to this and become either clingy or withdrawn. On the other hand, it is fair to say that some people don't realise that anything is wrong until the day when the other says, 'It's over and I'm leaving.'

Chapter 2

The Importance of Feelings and Recognising the Stages, Phases and Tasks of Grieving

Regardless of whether we are the one who wants to leave or the one who is left behind, feelings will play an important part in how we handle a separation, and, in fact, in how we handle our lives in general. Feelings feed our thoughts and subsequent actions, and they tell us how we are at any given time. Some of us are naturally more sensitive to feelings than others. As children, we may have been encouraged to express our feelings and may even have learned how to describe them. On the other hand, our feelings may have been ignored or discouraged; perhaps not directly, but somehow we have picked up the message that they're not okay or important. Consequently, we learn to keep them under wraps, and over time they may become hidden, even from ourselves.

When we experience loss, especially a loss like separation, our feelings become heightened and can lie very close to the surface. Crying is a natural way for the body to express emotions such as joy, sadness, excitement, frustration or anger. Many people say they feel much better after a good cry. Yet not everyone can shed tears; they are often seen as a sign of weakness instead of an important way for the body to express *and* release emotion. Sighing is also another body response that is a reaction to feelings, especially during a mourning period.

This chapter highlights the common feelings that are experienced throughout the journey of separation. These are also mentioned in other chapters in this book in the context of the various stages of that journey. Such feelings are by no means the only emotions that will be experienced during a separation, nor do they have to be the exact feelings that you will have if you are going through a separation – human beings are so unique that each person will experience their own journey in their own way. Feelings do not have a straightforward path, for example, relief doesn't always follow anger. Rather, different feelings come in and out, depending on what's happening at the time. The world outside us will often dictate our mood anyway. Although we may have been holding it together up until then, something gets triggered inside us as an intense feeling appears from nowhere and the floodgates open. Tears can be uncomfortable and even frightening, especially when they cannot be controlled or when we are in the company of other people. Tears might last for several minutes or hours and we are exhausted afterwards. But later a sense of calm descends once again. The very nature of grieving also can mean that sometimes when we think that one stage of grieving is finished we can roll back into it once again without warning. Do not despair; it will pass and you will get better at dealing with it.

What you can expect is that your grief has no time limit but usually is longer than you think. It takes more energy than you could have imagined, and will change over the course of the journey. It will become evident in other aspects of your life and you may feel the loss of other less important things in your life more acutely at this time. You are not only grieving for what has already been lost but also for what you had expected for your future as your wishes and dreams for your lives together come to an end. You can also expect that unresolved issues from your past come knocking at your door once again (such as rejection, anxiety and abandonment) and that your identity, the very core of your being, is now confused, leaving you with a sense of not knowing who you are anymore. The confusion and pain that is experienced by separating/separated people can be so preoccupying that they neglect themselves and they feel like they are going crazy at times. As they progress through the grief, they notice they are changing as people and they may seem (both to others and themselves) that they are behaving differently. They may also begin to search for meaning and purpose and their attitudes to things like religion or other philosophies take on a new perspective. Grief has a physical manifestation too and they may notice aches and pains that were not there before or feel like a limb has been amputated. You may put on or lose weight as you work your way through your grief. Certain dates or anniversaries can trigger off the grief once again making you wonder will you ever get over it. Others may not understand what you are experiencing and they may expect you to be over it sooner than you really are. You may find that, as the years pass, you have moved on emotionally, physically and practically and may have even remarried, but when you find yourself in another situation where loss is felt, you can remember your separation and experience pain once again. (Rando 1991)

There are various frameworks for looking at the experience of grief. We can see it in *stages* where the individual experiences the journey of *denial, anger, bargaining, depression* and *acceptance* (Kübler-Ross and Kessler 2005). We can also view it in *task format* as described by Worden (1991). He defines it as having four main tasks, namely *to accept the reality of the loss, to work through the pain of grief, to adjust to a new environment without the person* and *to emotionally relocate the missing person and move on with our lives.* Another way to explore the experience of grief is to look at it as Rando's (1991) three phases: the *avoidance phase* where we recognise the loss; the *confrontation phase* where we react to the separation, recall and re-experience what has been lost and begin to let go of the attachment to our ex-partner, realising the relationship really is over; and finally the *accommodation phase* where we move on and start investing in our new lives.

The Complexity of Grieving

Even if we know logically that a relationship wasn't working, we can still have contradictory feelings like sadness and anger that it is at an end.

We can feel controlled or even trapped by feelings, and they can block us from letting go if we become fixated or stuck, and we remain in pain. If you clench your fist and keep clenching it even when it is hurting you, eventually the pain will become agonising. For example, unresolved anger can lead to bitterness. Bitterness can be provoked when we see others happy whilst we are in the depths of our own sadness. If we are bitter, we can constantly blame others for our own frustration. Bitterness can eat away at us if it gets a hold, and it can take a lot of energy to maintain it. Although hard to detect because it starts its life off quietly, the roots of bitterness are deep and are nourished by frustration, anger, jealousy and resentment.

Difficulty in letting feelings go can also be because of something that happened at an earlier time in our lives. This may have left us with a wound that didn't quite heal and somewhere inside us we still hold the memory of that hurt.

John (37) recently separated from Sheila (38) when he found out she was having an affair. There had been a distance growing between them for some years and the affair was the tipping point for him to decide that the relationship was over. Even though he was the one to formally end it (although he would have argued that she was the one to finish it by being with someone else), he found himself constantly angry at her, looking at every little thing she did as trying to get back at him for leaving. In the end, one of his friends pointed out that his anger was affecting his other relationships and he decided to get some professional help.

Initially, with his counsellor, he continued to vent his anger and push the blame onto his ex-wife, but when his counsellor asked him had he ever felt angry like this before, he recalled a time when he was eight and his own dad had just left his mum. He was an only child and because his mum had been dealing with her own grief, it seemed to him that no one had really cared about his upset and confusion. It seemed to him that one day his dad was there and the next day he just disappeared. Being a small boy, he didn't have the language for or any concept of what was happening at the time. In counselling, he became aware of his own feelings of abandonment; lying under all the anger was a deep sadness that his family had broken up while he was so young. He admitted that he was horrified that what happened to him could still affect him because he hadn't thought about it in years. But he did begin to notice that over the following week he was calmer, even admitting to feeling relief. He could then allow himself to start feeling sad and more accepting of what had happened between himself and his ex-wife.

Because he became less consumed by such powerful and seemingly dormant emotions, which had been buried in his unconscious since childhood, he could then start exploring more clearly and calmly some of the patterns of behaviour that had contributed to the breakdown of his own marriage. He was able to do it without blaming or criticising anyone, including himself.

Experiences and Stages of Relationship Breakdown

So what do people experience when they are going through and moving beyond separation? Does everyone have the same experience? Is there a sequence to be followed?

Just over a decade ago, divorce became legalised in Ireland. In spite of this, there is still some stigma, although less so than before, attached to separating and/or divorcing. Separated people may tell themselves, 'I'm damaged goods. Who would want me now?' or 'I'm no good at relationships', or 'I'm too old to know how to begin my life again.' A sense of personal failure can run deep within the human soul. The end of a relationship that didn't work out can bring up shame and embarrassment and this is further compounded by having to tell other people what has happened. We might wonder what other people think of us. We worry about how people will react to the fact that we are no longer in a couple. This is not helped by the social stigma that still exists.

If we don't tell anyone about our worries, we run the risk of isolating ourselves while we struggle to maintain some sense of self-esteem in recovering from such a significant loss. We are also trying to establish, even if it is reluctantly, our place in the world as a single person. Although we are never the property of anyone else, being part of a couple does give us a sense of belonging. The loss of our couple status becomes particularly poignant when we have to fill in forms and are asked for our marital status, or when we sign greeting cards, omitting our ex-partner's name. This can start the grieving feelings all over again. Similar to a person who is bereaved through death, please do not feel obliged to send greeting cards in the first year following separation, or at least until you feel ready to do so.

Because separation is such a time of turmoil, we are more likely to become forgetful and lose track of time. We may fail to turn up for appointments as a result. This is because the feelings at this time are so strong that they overwhelm everything else. Routines are cast aside and normal day-to-day commitments are forgotten while mourning takes place. If you find yourself in the position of having obligations that must be fulfilled, make sure you record or make note of these each time so that you will remember – forgetting can just heighten anxiety. Put off what can be delayed until such time as you are ready to face the world again.

Separation is a time of huge change and unrest in a person's life; it's a period of unpredictability and you never know how you're going to feel from one day to the next. All you can be sure of is that life is different now. In order to help you through this time and to normalise the seemingly abnormal, I am highlighting some of the more general experiences of separating people, integrating the phases, stages and tasks that they face along the way.

Denial

In the early stages of separation, it is quite common to experience no feelings at all or a certain numbness, as if you've been given an anaesthetic. While an anaesthetic protects us from physical pain, this feeling of numbness is an important defence mechanism shielding us from being overwhelmed by emotional pain. We may know that the relationship is over but somehow we don't quite believe it. However, like all anaesthetics, this does wear off and other feelings – anger, panic, fear/anxiety, rejection, guilt, depression, loneliness, relief – begin to creep into our consciousness.

Denial is a way for our psyche to help us. When we wake up in the morning (if we have managed to get some sleep), for a few seconds we are protected from what's happened. Everything is okay in that brief time, until we become more awake and aware of our reality and of what's happened. Some people cannot access their emotions so easily – perhaps because they are afraid they will lose control – so they can experience this numbness for longer. Some feelings can be very painful, but the good thing is that they can become less so if they are allowed expression. The danger of not grieving is that any trapped emotions can manifest themselves as physical ailments and, subsequently, our health becomes affected, for example, we get headaches, unexplained pains in the body, stiffness in the joints, stomach upsets, and so on.

Separation means many other potential losses too – loss of friends, family, home, financial well-being, and so on. When we experience a further loss down the line, it is quite possible that the earlier loss will hit us with an unprecedented intensity that can make the particular issue at hand more overwhelming. When we are vulnerable and our defences are down, our earlier grief, which we have not dealt with, can then see an ideal opportunity to 'sneak in the door' and demand attention.

Anger

Anger is a natural feeling that occurs as part of grieving. It usually tells us that something is the matter and can mask other emotions, like fear and sadness, which may be more unbearable. However, it does carry with it a 'charge' that gives us an energy or impetus to detach from our partner. We can be angry with ourselves if we believe we are to blame, and/or angry with our partner for letting it happen. We can even be angry with God for putting us through such misery and we may ask the question, 'What did I do to deserve this?' Unfortunately, it can also be quite destructive if expressed inappropriately. It's quite common for anger to remain hidden in the initial stages, just after the decision has been made to separate. One party may be feeling guilty and that they have no right to get annoyed; the other will keep their anger suppressed because, if they want their partner to stay, they may be frightened of scaring him or her away.

However, by avoiding our anger we can become like a pressure cooker and, sooner or later, most of us will let off steam. Anger can leave us with a sense of being out of control if we keep it inside too long; the danger is that it could manifest itself through violence, which is explored in more detail in Chapter 6.

The anger that is experienced in separation is a unique type of anger that is hard to understand unless you have been through it yourself. You may have watched television programmes or heard a story about someone who has been left by their partner and they go to extreme measures to get revenge – by pouring paint over a prized Porsche or damaging their ex's property or possessions. To the outside world, this can look like madness. But separated people will say that, even if they wouldn't take such actions themselves, they do understand the anger and hurt behind them.

Unexpressed anger can affect us physically and mentally – we run the risk of becoming depressed as we 'stamp down' what is a very natural feeling, or else we can become sick when our body begins to protest at not being able to express itself. One lady admitted to me that she hadn't even realised she was angry until she noticed that there were lots of irritated people around her that day. It just took a simple question put to her by a friend – 'Are you angry yourself because you seem quite sensitive to it at the moment?' – before she realised that that she was in fact outraged by her husband's departure.

Other people may not be comfortable with your anger either. They may not recognise that it is a natural part of grieving that helps you to deal with pain. It is perfectly alright to feel angry – why wouldn't you feel that way? You are experiencing the loss of a significant relationship in your life. Try saying, 'I'm cross. I'm angry. I'm furious!' over and over into the mirror. Notice your tone of voice as you say it. Do you say it calmly or does your tone match the feelings of anger? Now say it slightly louder. Does your facial expression change? Do you notice any changes in your body? It might be a good idea to have a pillow nearby – you can use this to vent your anger, instead of damaging property or, even worse, causing hurt to yourself!

Not getting angry can cause people to remain stuck in the grieving process – that's how powerful anger is. It prolongs something that's very painful. If you find yourself uncomfortable with your own anger, or you can't get past being angry and you are not moving on, it is likely that it is time to see a professional who can help you.

Bargaining

Bargaining in the separation process always reminds me of making deals, usually with God or someone who can smooth the way for us to get the ideal result, for example, 'Hey God, if

31

you give me this, I promise that ...'. In the same way, with relationships, we can promise our partner that we'll change if only they'll stay. The pain that is brought on by the thought of our partner leaving can seem unbearable. We just want things to go back to the way they were before. This stage in the cycle of loss occurs when a person is still in some denial about the relationship being over for their partner. They still have hope that the relationship can continue and want to hang on. Lurking in their mind is a genuine uncertainty that the other will actually leave them and they will promise anything in order to maintain the status quo. Sometimes, at this point, a couple may actually decide to stay together under the premise of 'the devil you know is better than the devil you don't.' But are they staying together because they really want to be with each other or out of fear of being on their own? Will a separation be something that is just too hard to carry out? Another bargaining chip, more commonly expressed by the person who wants the relationship to end, is that they want to stay in touch, have lunch, be friends, and so on. These promises, although well-meaning, come from feelings of guilt and may be the leaver's way of trying to smooth the path to separation.

Bargaining, therefore, can be seen as that interim stage, when we've moved on from the initial shock but haven't yet really faced the reality (and the accompanying feelings) of what's happening, similar to the anaesthetic wearing off when there is still some numbness. Yet we are also aware that we are about to experience pain but, as of yet, we are unsure exactly how much suffering is to come.

Guilt and Rejection

No two people will come to the decision to separate at the same time. Consequently, there will usually be one person in a couple who does the leaving and one who will be left behind. Both will experience strong feelings, and guilt and rejection is part of this emotional load. The person who wants to leave experiences the greatest pain *prior* to the end of the relationship, whereas the person who is left behind is more likely to experience pain *after* being told that the relationship is over. This is discussed in more detail in Chapter 6.

The person who is leaving will often feel guilty at being the cause of so much pain. It may have taken them quite a long time to eventually decide that separation is the best solution. Because of religious beliefs, children, what others will think or the promise of a lifelong commitment to their partner, they may feel terrible at the thought of leaving the relationship.

Guilt can be crippling and can affect our ability to make decisions. Friends and family may try to persuade us to stay in a relationship and, even if it seems logical and practical to remain, somehow we feel dead inside and hopeless about any future happiness with our partner. However, to continue to act from guilt will, sooner or later, breed resentment, which is destructive in a relationship. Whether you decide to stay or to leave is your decision. You own it. Whatever decision you make carries responsibility and the decision to leave can be a huge burden. Making such a serious choice can seem easier if the blame is laid squarely on the shoulders of your partner for why you can't stay or because you believe it is better for your children. This is not taking responsibility, even if you feel fully justified. It does take quite considerable courage to leave, to look at all your options and to develop clarity behind your reasons for leaving. In some circumstances, there may be no option but to leave, for example, if the relationship has become violent or your partner has an affair that you deem unforgivable. These might be reasons that you can stand behind even if you have ambivalent feelings about the direction you take. You are taking responsibility by saying, 'I cannot stay because I cannot forgive him/her' rather than, 'He/she did this and that's why I'm leaving' because, in reality, violence and affairs happen in intimate relationships and are not irreparable issues in all cases (Gurman and Jacobson, 2002).

Once the news of the separation has sunk in, the person who is left is likely to be devastated. As the initial shock wears off, it can be replaced by strong feelings of rejection. They might blame themselves and ask questions such as: 'How could you pick him/her over me?', 'Why wasn't I good enough?' and 'What did I do wrong and what can I do to fix it?' Or they might even say, 'That's it, I'm useless at relationships.' They may try to overcompensate by being the best partner/mother/father/friend/employee to prove that they are worthy. Yet that feeling of rejection is still there. It becomes worse if they can see their partner getting on with their lives while they remain stuck and now really feel like a failure. Yet, they haven't failed – they were in a relationship that didn't work out, probably for lots of reasons. They may have been responsible for some of what went wrong but their partner also had a part to play.

If you are in this situation, it is quite normal to feel rejected and for what's happened to make a huge dent in your self-esteem (your sense of value or worth). What is not healthy is to continue to hold on to the notion of not being good enough or feeling like you've failed as this could possibly cripple your ability to be happy in the future. You are worthy of giving and receiving love and, even if you are right now wallowing in the throes of huge hurt and self-blame at being left, you have a choice as to whether this defines who you are as a person or whether you see it as a particularly painful experience in the context of one particular relationship.

A healthy way for many people to deal with their damaged self-esteem and confidence (what you believe you are capable of) is to explore what went wrong with their relationship, dismantling the problems and how they might have contributed to them, and discover what they would like to be different in a new relationship down the road. They will often discover that they now have needs and values that were different to before, both as a result of their separation and also because they are now more mature and at a different life stage. This clarity and awareness can help them to avoid the pitfalls of repeating some of the more problematic patterns that may have been destructive in the old relationship.

Rebuilding self-esteem and confidence is an important part of moving on and taking back some semblance of personal power and control over your own life. Although not for everybody, many separated people find they become more interested in themselves as people, and take part in self-development workshops or groups as a result.

Fear

Fear and anxiety can hit us at any point on the journey. Indeed, they may strike us many times and, for some, they may always be there in the background. As the reality of our situation hits home, the uncertainty of our future can become apparent. This uncertainty has to do with more than just the loss of our partner, as mentioned earlier. We may ask ourselves: 'What's going to happen to me now?', 'Where will I live?', 'Will I have to move out of the neighbourhood?', 'Will there be enough money?', 'Who will take care of me if I get ill?', 'How will we manage the children?' or even, 'Will I lose contact with my children altogether?' These are very real concerns and of course they will bring up varying degrees of anxiety, based on their level of importance.

Prior to the decision to separate, there is a period when we will consider our options. Even if things aren't great, will it be worse if we leave? Or will we stay because we're too frightened to leave? What kind of life is ahead of us in this case? This 'to-and-fro' thinking, or ambivalence, can continue for a considerable period of time. Experiencing almost polar opposite feelings can make the decision a hard one. You might find yourself loving and hating your partner in the same breath. Ambivalence brings about plenty of confusion, which is why people will say that it's hard to make decisions during and after separation. Some people naturally vacillate and find any decision hard to make, but the journey of separation is one of those periods where ambivalent feelings are ever-present and where fear is generally at the root of them.

Panic attacks occur when the body is literally gripped by an overwhelming sense of fear and manifest themselves by shortness of breath, a dry throat, a pounding heart, sweating, shaking or trembling all over, and nausea. They can strike out of the blue, even when you're asleep. A panic attack is a frightening thing to happen to anyone, especially when you've never experienced it before. A couple of panic attacks may be nothing serious and simply symptomatic of fear, but if you find that they keep coming back it would be advisable to see your doctor.

Relief

When the separation finally happens, either the initial conversation when one tells the other they want to leave or when a couple physically separates, i.e. when one or both move out, or when the papers are signed, it can come with quite a profound and surprising sense of relief. Tension may have been building for some time. A couple may have had several conversations about what's happening and why the relationship isn't working, or they may even try to work on the relationship to see if it's worthwhile remaining together. Finally, there comes a point where there is no going back and the only thing to do is to separate. The slack now loosens the tug-of-war rope and there is no longer a push-and-pull tension between them.

Although it is not possible to give a definitive answer to how each individual child will react to their parents' separation, research shows us that, even though they may not want their family to break up, children in families where there is parental conflict will often feel relief because they believe that the tension has now come to an end. For these children, when they are told the news it can seem like a storm has broken and they are no longer holding their breath, waiting for the next bolt of lightning to strike.

They will still struggle with their lives and may take a year or two to re-adjust to what's happened but their recovery will be largely due to how their parents handle their separation from each other. Such a change can help children to build resilience and the majority of children do not have psychological problems as a result, but they will nevertheless be able to recall 'painful memories, troublesome feelings and ongoing concerns about their families' (Emery and Sbarra 2002, p. 512). How they adapt is helped by a close relationship with at least one parent, but preferably both, and being kept away from their parents' issues with each other, i.e. they aren't caught up in the adult experience of separation.

Loneliness and Depression

As part of our grief, the flood of feelings we experience can be overwhelming. Although no one wants to experience pain, and certainly not for long periods, nature has a way of helping us along by shutting down our nervous system until we can gather enough energy to deal with the aftermath. The grieving feelings that come with any loss are heavy and we may wonder at times, 'What's the point in going on?' We might think, 'I can't be bothered getting out of bed' or 'Life seems hopeless.' We struggle with trying to pull ourselves out of this state and others may also be alarmed that we have lost the spring in our step and may also be doing their best to help us snap out of it, eventually becoming frustrated when we don't, thus increasing our isolation. Everyone, including ourselves, can become alarmed if this happens.

Kübler-Ross and Kessler invite the question: '... ask yourself whether the situation you're in is actually depressing. The loss of a loved one is a very depressing situation and depression is a normal and appropriate response. To not experience depression ... would be unusual.' (2005, p. 21) This type of depression is a reaction to what has happened and is different to clinical depression, which is a long-term and excessive depressed state. When someone recognises and does not try to push away this reactive depression, and instead they allow it to be part of their experience, Kübler-Ross and Kessler believe that it can 'allow the sadness and emptiness to cleanse you and help you explore your loss in its entirety ... and will leave you as soon as it has served its purpose' (2005, p. 22).

However, normal depression can turn into clinical depression if it goes on for a long period and may need medical intervention. So if you feel you are at this stage, try to record every day how you are feeling or ask a trusted friend or family member to keep an eye on you. It is a bit of a balancing act because it is quite normal and is a healthy part of moving on for us to feel a deep, deep sadness and despair for a while.

> Muiris (52): I didn't know I could sink so low and feel so defeated. I was okay for a while and was managing. But one night, when I was out, all I could see were other couples getting on with each other and I realised that I didn't have that anymore. It was like a cold slap on the face. I nearly ran out of the place and didn't go to work the following day. In fact, I didn't even bother getting up that day or the next. I just wanted it all to go away and to sleep my way out of it. For the next ten days, I felt like a zombie, not really feeling anything. I couldn't care less what happened to me really.
>
> My daughter noticed that something was wrong. I couldn't even begin to describe how I was feeling but I guess it was all there in my eyes because she put her arms around me and held me while the tears fell and I sobbed like a small child. It didn't seem right that she was the one who had to be the parent in charge, soothing me, but there was nothing I could do but sit there and let her. I was all out of good intentions to accept what had happened and to be strong and brave ....

This sadness and emptiness can also bring the onset of loneliness as we face a new life as a single person. No one enters a relationship believing it will bring them loneliness – they expect it will be the other way around. They are, perhaps, hoping that they have found that perfect someone with whom they will have a deep connection and with whom they will stay close forever.

When we find a partner and they do not live up to our expectations of this permanent closeness, the relationship itself becomes lonely. When our partner disappoints us by not understanding and meeting our needs over a long period of time we can become disappointed and start distancing ourselves from them either emotionally, sexually or by involving ourselves in other activities such as work, child-rearing, sport and so on. So, part of the relief that can be felt at the time of separation can be to do with the end of loneliness *in* a relationship.

However, the aftermath of a relationship can bring about a different kind of loneliness; you may be lonely for your ex-partner, missing your children when they are with their other parent or missing the life you had altogether as a family. If we have lost something, we become anxious and the level of anxiety we feel is dependent on the value or meaning what we are losing has for us. One of the greatest fears about separating is that experience of loneliness – it can intensify the already present feeling of failure. If we know this loss to be permanent, rather than something that is temporary, and that there is no way back, a sense of despair sets in and we become vulnerable to our own worry and sadness.

Even if we haven't felt an emotional closeness to our partner for a long time, at least he or she was there at mealtimes, and shared a home, a bed, holidays, finances and parenting with us. Loneliness tells us we are quite separate from someone. Our response to the fear of it can be to find excuses to see or stay in contact with our ex-partner in order to give us a sense of connectedness. The thought of being alone can be unbearable. Even keeping busy can be seen as avoiding the loneliness or emptiness that faces us when the other is gone.

Quite a lot of energy can be invested in tip-toeing around loneliness. Perhaps we have never really been by ourselves before. Some people avoid loneliness entirely by starting a new relationship straight away. This is motivated not so much by really liking and respecting a new partner, but rather out of fear of being on our own. If you are identifying with not ever wanting to be on your own, ask yourself what you are afraid of exactly. Is it that, by being with someone else, you feel you are somehow worthy of being in a relationship – 'If someone else likes me, then I am good enough?' Or does it give you security in some shape or other, either financial or emotional? Or is it just that you want your home to contain someone else besides yourself? Nowadays, we have technology that helps us stay connected with the rest of the world and gives us a sense that we're not so much on our own. With Facebook, Twitter, dating websites, chat rooms and so on, we can while away the hours, often pleasantly so. This does not, however, replace face-to-face interaction with another human being.

Part of the task at this point of the journey is to face up to, and become comfortable with, being by yourself. Those who have done this will often say that, once they've adjusted, it's not a problem anymore for them. Yes, they will feel lonely from time to time, but this is usually only for short periods. In fact, they often find comfort in solitude and can please themselves. They discover, perhaps for the first time, what they truly enjoy rather than what their partner likes; they are no longer focusing on meeting their partner's needs. If there are no children or other dependents in the relationship, they no longer have to make plans with someone else in mind.

Acceptance and Letting Go

In the early stages of separation, a lot of our emotional and physical energy is taken up with grieving and trying to deal with the practicalities that come with the end of a relationship. We can't stop thinking about it. It consumes us and we find it hard to concentrate and find time for the other parts of our lives. Our feelings are intense and they can sap the life from us for what can appear like an interminable stretch. We find ourselves hitting a low point and can feel quite depressed, as described above. We may have quite good days and believe we are getting over it and then hit a bad patch and wonder will we ever get over it.

Eventually, if we don't get stuck somewhere along the way, we start to let go and move on a little bit at a time. Holding onto habits, such as calling or texting our ex regularly, means that we are still holding on to the relationship. Perhaps we aren't ready to let go yet and it's okay to acknowledge that this is where we are right now. Please do not confuse letting go and accepting the situation with being okay with it; maybe you will never be alright about your relationship ending. It just means that you are now finding yourself acknowledging a new reality, that there is no going back. Instead, you start taking deliberate and practical steps to move forward. You begin to re-position your ex-partner in the context of your life. Where once they played a central or key figure in your day-to-day life, they are now placed further away from you – you cannot forget them or ignore them entirely, but they no longer feature in such a dominant way. You may notice that you find yourself removing some of the things that remind you of them. If you are the one who has left the home, you begin to take steps to ensure that your identity is removed from the home, such as redirecting post, removing all belongings and so on. Dealing with the practical things, even if it is difficult, does help you to detach emotionally. In addition, doing new things without your ex, such as trying something new or going on the type of holiday that really wouldn't have interested them, can help you to live in the present and can actually be quite enjoyable. Yes, you may miss your ex and feel wobbly without them at times, but allow yourself to feel that way for a short while and then get back to enjoying yourself as best you can.

Over time, you will begin to be less bothered about what your ex is getting up to in his or her life. You might notice that the emotions you feel when you think of them are less troublesome than they used to be. Some people say that when the worst of the pain passed they eventually felt a kind of compassion for their partner, which is not about wanting them back, but more about putting the past to rest.

41

Throughout the journey of separation, from the initial moment when the decision to separate has been contemplated through to the acceptance phase, feelings will move back and forth. They alternate – one day we can feel glad that the separation has happened and feel like we've moved on, and the next we land right back in a sad and bad place. For some, there may be a sense of despair as they wonder if they will ever get past it. This is a natural part of the process and usually passes. Just remember that when you experience a good day and then get knocked back, you are still aware that it is possible to have good days because you've already had one (or more) in spite of what's happened. What can help is to make a note of your moods in your diary or calendar – you might be quite surprised at how many good days you have as time goes on. Our minds have a tendency to distort our experiences, when in reality it might be rather different. Do we say to ourselves, 'It's terrible *all* the time; I haven't had one good moment' when, actually, we may have had a fun night out or something good happened at work, or we had a constructive chat with someone. A useful clue as to whether you are distorting reality might be how frequently you use the words 'always' and 'never'.

Another good thing about keeping a diary is that it can also be helpful to record the day's events and to look over them a few weeks later. People who do this can be surprised at how their feelings and perspectives change over short periods of time. People who have gone on to re-build their lives can usually recall the time of separation as difficult and even devastating, but can't really engage with the feelings of that time. For example, they are able to recall being angry at the time, and to talk about it, without actually feeling remnants of that anger because they have actually moved on and no longer feel that way.

How Can We Help Our Feelings?

Feelings are like small children who cling to our legs until we pay attention to them. Many counsellors or therapists will hear their clients say, 'I just want the pain to go away – fix it please', believing the professional to have a magic wand that will banish painful feelings. If a small child believes he or she is being listened to and understood, is treated kindly and with compassion, sooner or later they will calm down, feel better and will go back to play once more. The reason why therapy is helpful is because the skill of the counsellor or therapist is to encourage the client to slow down everything and allow their feelings to run their course. People who have the courage to stay with their feelings without rushing them on or surfing over them usually find they begin to gain more control over their feelings rather than the other way around. They are less likely to remain stuck in their grief and maintain a healthy sense of themselves and their needs.

Even if you never seek professional help, you can still provide internal space into which you can invite your feelings, one at a time. You can connect with what's happening in a powerful way through a focusing technique, which was developed by philosopher and psychologist Eugene Gendlin. This technique can be tried either on your own or with someone you trust. If you want to try it on your own, make sure you will be undisturbed for at least half an hour. It might seem strange or awkward at first and it may seem like you have to wait for ages until something comes, but just be patient.

Take about a minute or two to grow quiet inside and focus on your breathing, bringing your awareness to the middle of your body, the part between your throat and your abdomen, where you usually feel emotions, and take some time to get a sense of how you are. When you begin to notice you have a clearer sense of yourself, you have created that space inside from which to listen to your feelings. Now, ask yourself:

What is the main thing for me now?

or

What needs my attention most at the moment?

or

What do I feel as I recall a particular situation in my life right now? [*Pause.*]

Ask yourself how you are carrying the answer to any of these questions in your body and take time to become aware of the feeling or sensation that is there right now (e.g. a dryness in the throat, a tightness in the chest or an all-over feeling of anxiety, fear, anger or discomfort). Wait until something comes.

As you sense what is there, how it is felt in your body, ask yourself if it is okay for you to just stay with what's there in a gentle, caring and compassionate way, just to be with it the way it is right now and notice what it is like to do that ... giving it space to be just the way it is, space to breathe .... [*Pause.*]

Invite a word, phrase, image or memory to come into your awareness that fits the way you are feeling about the problem or issue right now and wait for your body to respond.

Welcome what comes now ... moving back and forth between the word or image and the felt sense (the sensation in your body) to check if they match exactly. Notice what has changed, even a little bit, allowing yourself time to feel the sense of change and what is new for a while, protecting yourself from any critical inner voice wanting to come into this special space. [*Pause.*]

As you stay with whatever sensation is there, notice if there is anything more it wishes to tell you right now. [*Pause.*] If there is more, start another round of focusing with the new felt sense that is there now.

If there isn't anything more, ask yourself if it is okay to stop, at least for now. Pause and wait ....

Note what you want to remember from this session, and ask yourself: What has changed now? What is different now? [*Pause.*]

Stay with the body feel for a little while longer, nurturing the change you are aware of right now. If you notice there is anything unfinished or incomplete about what you are feeling in your body, gently mark the place, letting it know you will give it attention another time.

44

Finally, thank your body for the unique way it is speaking to you today, letting it know more of your story, letting you feel more at one with yourself and letting you know how you are in the flow of life.

Slowly and gently, bring your awareness back into the room.

If you find it impossible to sit still and be quiet in yourself, another way to manage strong upsetting feelings is by doing something, such as clearing out the cupboards or tidying the garden. This is because by doing something physical and completing a task that will affect your life for the better, you are grounding yourself or taking yourself out of your 'busy' head. This, in itself, can help to lift a person's mood. Although the earlier feeling is still there, its intensity will have diminished. Sometimes, even a slight shift in the feeling allows the mind to clear a little and often this is enough to get over the hump. Some people find that when they list out what they've done during the day, they feel a sense of achievement and are in a more positive frame of mind.

Feelings and Gender

Grief is such an individual experience and no two people will mourn in exactly the same manner. Although men and women have similar processes of grief, similar needs and similar feelings, they can deal with them in entirely different ways. In her book *How to Go on Living When Someone You Love Dies*, grief expert Therese Rando recognises this and says:

> One of the worst problems that occurs in grief but is totally unnecessary is the increased pain, misunderstanding, frustration, and secondary losses that you may have to experience if you fail to understand the difference between your responses and those of someone else you love who is a member of the other sex. (1991, p. 64)

There are many factors that will influence how people grieve, but a key component is our gender conditioning. Although society is changing to integrate our responses to be less stereotypical and more androgynous or neutral, e.g. we now encourage men to cry and women to become more independent, we are still influenced by more traditional gender stereotypes that form the roadmap to how we deal with our feelings and experiences in life. Our family, society and culture will largely determine how we perceive our roles as boys and girls and later on as men and women, but we are also hardwired biologically to deal with life in a different manner. The way in which each gender is programmed to manage problems is entirely different. For example, a man may react quickly in order to find a solution, whereas a woman may want to explore her feelings, express them and have them acknowledged by others. That does not mean that men are without feelings or women without logical reasoning and ability to take action; it just means that they may be naturally more inclined to resolve their difficulty in different ways. The most important thing to remember is that because of our uniqueness as human beings we should not pigeonhole ourselves into a way of dealing with our grief: 'I should/shouldn't be feeling this way', 'I should be over this by now' or 'this is not normal.'

Taking on board the differences between the genders, the next two chapters will describe how men and women, generally speaking, deal with separation and their priorities when their relationship ends. The purpose of these chapters is to help you understand how your gender may be affecting your response to separation. Not all of it may be relevant and you may recognise some of the opposite gender traits in yourself (i.e. if you are a man, some of the characteristics that accompany feminine grief may be familiar to you and vice versa). There is nothing abnormal or wrong about this. The main thing is that you gain more recognition and understanding of your feelings at this difficult time. Reading these chapters may also help you to understand your partner's possible motivations and feelings.

Chapter 3

Women and Separation

Marina (38): 'When I found out that my partner had been having an affair, it devastated me. I had dropped all my friends and barely kept contact with my family just so I could spend all my free time with him. He was so busy at work and was doing well career wise. We decided that I would stop work when we discovered I was pregnant. I never thought those late nights (at the office or out at a client dinner) after our baby was born were the times he'd begun an affair with a colleague. Being so busy with motherhood, I didn't notice that he no longer wanted to be near me ... just thought that it was one of those things that everyone talks about when you have a baby. By the time I noticed it, it was too late. He was already in love with someone else and had decided to leave me and our daughter.'

Although people break up for lots of reasons, many relationships come apart at the seams because of the couple's failure to recognise their gender differences. They experience these differences as irritations or deliberate acts to avoid, punish, dominate or control the other, as described in more detail in Chapter 1.

The female could be described as the emotional container in a relationship. More often than not, research tells us that a woman is more sensitive to the emotional undercurrents in a relationship than her male partner and becomes aware sooner if there are problems, that something isn't quite right. She is predisposed (biologically, psychologically and through cultural conditioning) to remain in touch with her feelings and to respond to them.

Leading research scientist on marriage and family John Gottman describes how the female evolved with the ability to calm herself quickly in the face of threat, so that she could still continue to produce milk for her offspring and ensure their survival. According to Gottman and Silver (2007, p. 37), 'any nursing mother can tell you, the amount of milk you produce is affected by how relaxed you feel, which is related to the release of oxytocin in the brain. So natural selection would favour a female who could quickly soothe herself and calm down after feeling stressed.' Indeed, a woman may also have been raised to talk about her fears and anxieties without it being seen by her as a threat to her gender role.

Because of her natural nurturing quality (due to an abundance of oestrogen) a woman is more likely to feel comfortable directing herself towards the needs of others, often suppressing her own identity in deference to her relationships. This hormone is described by Patricia Allen in her book *Getting To I Do* as:

> an (affect) feeling hormone. It keeps women caring more about feelings and emotions than cars and jobs .... A woman who is influenced by her oestrogen processes her feelings and thoughts, which keeps her in constant touch with them so she can make a decision to move toward pleasure if she 'feels' good, or stop actions if she 'feels' bad. As this hormone level changes, so too will her ability to give selflessly. It may go partly to explain why a woman in her forties can become more assertive than at

a younger age. This in itself is not a bad thing – she may become more interested in doing things for herself like returning to education or returning to the workplace/ becoming more ambitious but it can also cause her to wonder with all this giving, what did she get back? (2002, p. 46)

A woman will most commonly leave a relationship because she is unhappy or is feeling neglected or unloved by her part-ner. Her unhappiness can be rooted in a belief that her partner no longer cares about her, that she doesn't matter to him or is not a priority in his life. She can feel as if he has abandoned her emotionally and physically if he is away from her a lot or chooses to do things that exclude her.

When a woman expresses her unhappiness, she can be met with a defensive response from her partner as he tries to protect himself from what he perceives as criticism (and, yes, men are particularly sensitive to not pleasing their woman). In truth, most women will say that they only want their partner to know that they are unhappy so they can do something about it together. John Gray, in his book *Men Are from Mars, Women Are from Venus*, says that Venusians (women) 'value love, commu-nication, beauty, and relationships. They spend a lot of time supporting, helping, and nurturing one another. Their sense of self is defined through their feelings and the quality of their relationships. They experience fulfilment through sharing and relating' (p. 18). As her focus is on connecting or relating to people, working as part of a team and 'relating to the needs of others', a woman may not realise that a man may become over-burdened by the responsibility (he believes he is responsible) to make it better. He wants to feel like he's a success with his part-ner, but when this becomes too difficult or too complicated, his own doubts set in about his ability to be able to solve the prob-lem. He may become critical or contemptuous of her, become abusive (emotionally and/or physically) or seem like he's not paying attention to her conversation by focusing on the screen of the laptop, television or PlayStation, or else do a disappearing act altogether, which will add to her frustration and lessen her feeling of closeness or connectedness to him.

As I mention in the next chapter, on men and separation, women are fortunate in one respect because they usually have a strong support structure in their friends and family to help them when times get tough. Women are good at empathising with each other. They understand each other and can communicate their understanding of one another's feelings. Rando would also say that society encourages women 'to be dependent and to look to others to assist them. The helplessness and powerlessness of grief is not incompatible with their role' (1991, p. 69). They do not conceal their feelings in the same way as men. However, some women, for whatever reason, may need permission from others to grieve, especially if they are angry, since anger remains a more accepted emotion in men than women.

Relationships are important to women because they give them a sense of purpose, of belonging, and, for some, a social status which may not be there otherwise. So, to have that disappear is very threatening for a woman. She may now be on her own with dependent children and feeling quite frightened about how she is going to manage. Or she might also feel fearful that her children might be taken away from her if she cannot cope.

The initial stages of separation are very upsetting for everyone. The woman's loss of her relationship may mean that she may have to start making decisions on her own and become more independent. If she is a mother, in the early days anyway, it may be unclear how, as part of a separated couple, she can continue to co-parent. She can worry that the children are not being taken care of properly when they are out of her care and spending time with their dad. When the dust settles, she may begin to understand that, actually, she may have a bit more free time when her ex has the children. Of course she will miss them terribly and, if most of her time was taken up with responding to her children's needs, she may not know what to do with a free evening, day or weekend. Her friends may all be in their own relationships and be busy doing other things and she may have little or no money to spend if she goes out. This can be a lonely time. However, if she is thinking positively, it might be the ideal opportunity for her to indulge in things that give her pleasure and delight as an individual. This may be as simple as having a bath on her own without anyone pulling at her – it's not about the bath; it's about the 'me' time. There's enough negativity spinning around inside her so it's important to balance this out with self-nurturing. This can be particularly difficult for a caring, giving woman who is more drawn towards putting others' needs before her own. The woman who is already in touch with what makes her feel good and is comfortable about receiving as well as giving is more likely to adjust better to the times when she is on her own.

When a woman gives to herself (and that also means receiving when someone wants to do something for her), she is likely to be happier and less anxious, more so than the woman who just gives, gives, gives. The person who gives too much becomes the doormat for everyone else, and it should come as no surprise that all that giving over the years becomes quite wearing with very little reward. Her identity becomes consumed by others' needs and not her own. So when separation happens, especially if the children are grown up, she is left with a very bleak question: 'Who am I anyway?'

How you deal with your separation can be influenced by whether you were the person who left or whether your partner left you. As mentioned earlier, the person who has been left by their partner, regardless of whether they are male or female, has very intense and uncomfortable feelings *after* they are told that the relationship is over. The person who leaves usually has these feelings *before* they declare that the relationship is over.

When Your Partner Leaves You – Self-Esteem

As small children, we sought our parents' approval. When they praised us and took us into their arms for cuddles and kisses, this told us that they loved us. We pick up messages from a very young age that determine our self-worth, i.e. you are only good if you behave yourself or come first in your class or at sports, etc., or good children share with their brothers and sisters, help Mammy, etc. We may have carried these messages with us to adulthood and only feel good when we are working from this script. There are many developmental tasks we are faced with as children, among them being able to soothe ourselves when we are upset and to develop an inner power or sense of worthiness that is not so influenced by others' opinions or beliefs, which are usually disguised in language such as 'should', 'must' and 'ought'.

Learning to harness a belief in our self-worth and to balance our emotions and frustrations are important for our well-being, without which we are at the mercy of the outside world where other people get to decide whether we are a good enough person.

As adults, we can look back at our childhoods with a (hopefully) mature understanding of when our parents may have been stressed, worn out or worried, and had little love, praise or attention to give us. But somewhere inside still lurks the vulnerable child seeking approval and acceptance, and when we feel rejected, our bodies experience the symptoms of that original rejection: butterflies in the tummy, dry mouth, tingling in the arms, even a kind of restlessness or nervousness.

Perhaps as a caregiver in adult life, we tend to others' needs as part of being a 'good' person, hoping we'll get the love back that we give out and also feel good about our generous giving. But many caregivers are not good receivers of others' caregiving and if it's all flowing one way (i.e. from them) also it can mean that the caregiver can end up feeling taken for granted. Many women approaching mid-life (with lowering oestrogen levels) find themselves feeling quite resentful – their efforts haven't been rewarded in quite the way they had hoped and they don't know how to deal with the disappointment. Do they complain and hope that someone will hear them or do they sweep it under the carpet and hope the feeling will go away?

The less nurturing woman whose life may have taken a different direction, and who has perhaps been very successful in her career, may also be faced with a sense of failure when her relationship ends, living as she does in a world where success means everything. Learning to suppress her own emotions over the years to survive in a competitive world may mean that she does not have the capacity or the resources in place for dealing with her grief now.

If your partner leaves you, you may be shocked in the beginning, but as this shock wears off you begin to wonder, 'What did I do wrong? Was it this? Was it that? If I do it differently, will they come back?' These are the frantic questions I've heard both women and men ask themselves when their partner leaves them. It's as if they feel they are to blame somehow and they were the ones who caused the relationship to end, that they weren't good enough. Their self-esteem may now be in pieces, albeit on a temporary basis.

When You Leave Your Partner – Guilt

If you were the one to end the relationship, you have a clearer idea about why you're leaving and what was wrong in the relationship. You have hopefully made efforts to address this with your ex before ultimately making your decision to leave.

Leaving is difficult for everyone, contrary to what people say. One might consider that, as the leaver, you have the easier side of things, but, for most, the decision is an agonising one and is particularly hard for people who would normally leave the decision making to others. It's also compounded by guilt at having hurt someone else, even if you don't love them anymore.

If you have children, you will also have to take into account what will happen to them. Will they blame you and hate you for splitting up their family? Or, even worse, will they want to go and live with your ex as a result? However, if staying meant continuing to be unhappy, at least leaving has given you a chance of happiness, either on your own or with someone else.

Some people feel they have no choice but to leave. They may have considered their options long and hard and arrived at a place where to separate is the only option. If your relationship is a violent one, it is most definitely not good to go back to your partner if he is not taking responsibility for the violence and getting help. This also applies if you are the perpetrator. To stay together will mean the likelihood of the abuse pattern repeating itself.

Life Stages

As mentioned in Chapter 2, the amount we grieve is dependent on the importance the relationship held for us and the expectations we had for that relationship. Our expectations can be linked with our age group and at what stage our relationship with our ex-partner was at.

Younger Women

It would seem reasonable to say that unrealistic ideas about marriage, poor communication skills and greater narcissism among young adults have contributed to the increase in early marital breakups. A successful (and by this I mean 'happy enough') relationship does require both parties to be realistic about what a long-term committed relationship means. It's not all a bed of roses and relationships do go through testing times. In fact, relationships need challenges from time to time in order to grow.

Sometimes a couple will experience one change after the other, for example, moving home (and away from friends and family in some cases) and job, and perhaps having a new baby. Each change has a psychological impact on us as individuals, which will consequently affect our relationship. A couple needs time to recover and re-adjust before the next change comes along. This might mean one person needs more support (togetherness) and the other needs space, so their needs may clash.

A younger woman who is involved in a relationship break-up may have been planning a long-term future with her partner, only to find that she has to face starting over again. She may want a family some day and worry that she'll never meet her Prince Charming. Sadly, some people's relationships have already run their course when they are young, but they are too afraid to leave their partner in case they won't meet anyone else. So they go on and get married because it's 'the next step' and they may secretly be hoping that it will inject something into their relationship to bring it back to life.

> Brid (32): 'We met in our early twenties and, although we'd travelled the world together, when it finally came to settling down my boyfriend just couldn't do it. He felt he was still too young and I felt ready to get engaged (at 31), get married and start our family. We had talked about it over the years and I thought it was only a matter of time. All my dreams lay in little pieces when we broke up. I feel I'm too old to meet someone new and go through all this again.'

As young children, one of the big challenges that faced us was how to handle frustration when our needs went unmet. Did we sulk openly or did we become silent? Or have we learned that it's alright to be disappointed, that perhaps it's not our partners who have let us down but our expectations?

Women still do feel pressure to meet a partner, fall in love, get married and have families. Even in this day and age, many women will admit they are quite traditional at heart and want to feel safe, secure and cherished by their partner. A woman who finds herself on her own at an age when she thought she'd be in a different place in her life can experience a lot of self-doubt – 'What if I never meet someone? My biological clock is ticking, I don't own my own home, my friends are all settling down and I feel like a spare wheel.'

Younger women with children will naturally incur the worry of having enough financially for themselves and their children. They may be nervous about how they will juggle their daily lives without their partner's input. Perhaps they have made career sacrifices to take up the ever-present and available role of homemaker. To have lost so much can make a person bitter if they dwell too long on their risk not having paid off. Unfortunately, they may be faced with the practical decision of having to go back to work, but are feeling de-skilled and lacking in confidence.

Women also worry about ageing and losing their attractiveness – in fact, they can become quite competitive with each other (although few will admit to this). The media and society in general feeds this insecurity, and when something like the end of a relationship happens, these feelings can be intensified. As each year goes by and a woman becomes a little bit older, she can worry about maintaining herself so she is still physically appealing and can find a mate who will commit to her long term.

Older Women

A woman facing separation in her more mature years is often better equipped emotionally to deal with the fallout than men of the same age. She is more likely to be closer to her children as a result of being the primary caregiver and can rely on them for support. Notwithstanding this, she may also be in the throes of dealing with, or has already dealt with, what is now commonly called 'empty nest syndrome' – a period of adjustment when all the children have left home and no longer need her mothering. This in itself is a significant life-stage adjustment as she finds herself faced with the loss of a role that may have taken up most of her adult and married life.

To be hit with a further loss when her relationship breaks up can seem an impossible endurance, even if she was the one to initiate the separation. Perhaps she had been looking forward to greater freedom and doing things with her partner that they couldn't do until their children became financially independent and left home. Although many disappointments in life can be attributed to unrealistic expectations, nevertheless, to find yourself in a broken relationship at a point in your life when you and your partner could be reaping the benefits of your hard work can seem like a difficult pill to swallow.

Life expectancy is now greater than it's ever been and many older women (at pre-retirement or retirement age) will say that they want to spend what time they have left being happy. Although no one likes to be on their own long term, unlike men, many older women are happier being single and don't want to start a new relationship, having perhaps spent a lifetime caring for others. It doesn't mean that they won't have periods of great loneliness – after all, they may have been used to being the centre of other people's lives – but they have better support structures in place to minimise any threat of becoming isolated. Even if a woman wants to end her relationship, she will have grown used to her ex-husband/partner's presence. Even if he wasn't physically around a lot of the time, his belongings will be a constant reminder of his place in her life. Thus, for a woman to find herself feeling that her future is bleak, especially in the initials stages of the physical separation, is quite natural and will more or less pass as she adjusts to her new life.

If her husband was the one to leave, especially when she was looking forward to spending more of her free time with him, this can seem like the ultimate betrayal. Much of her life may have revolved around him and she may feel that her life is now over. The loss of a husband (and not to death) can be particularly complex as she has built her life and family with him. She may also be harbouring the belief that this is just a mid-life crisis for him and he'll come back – it's impossible to grieve properly when there is still hope.

Financial hardship is often one of the most significant challenges of separation for both men and women, regardless of age. In the past, being financially dependent on her husband, coupled with the stigma (both social and religious) attached to marital break-up may have been strong enough reasons for a woman not to seek separation, but, of course, times have now changed. Although an older woman may not have to worry about custody of children, which would have been of primary concern in her younger years, being taken care of financially is still of paramount importance as her husband may have been the sole breadwinner. Even if she had worked, she may have taken time off to take care of children. Also, only in recent years has it become more commonplace for women to be afforded the same opportunities for promotion as men.

A separated woman may be able to manage her finances most of the time, but constantly worry about unpredictable expenses. If her husband had previously managed the financial side of married life, this becomes another new role to learn along with many others, such as technical jobs around the house. These things, although quite mundane, serve as constant reminders and can start a whole new wave of grieving.

If her partner has met someone new and there are family occasions coming up, being single is awkward. Everyone else is enjoying themselves and it can be impossible to join in. These occasions, while they can't be avoided, can become an endurance test for even the toughest of people. When any of these things happen, remind yourself that, although you might feel quite helpless, you may in reality be better at these things than you think. Friends and family are usually quite supportive and willing to help if you take the first step and reach out. And, remember, at social gatherings where your ex-partner is present you don't have to stay until the last guest has left. Make a promise to yourself a few days before that it is perfectly okay to stay for a couple of hours and then make your excuses. Although it doesn't take the pressure off entirely, what this promise will do is give you back some control over 'out-of-control' dread or anxiety.

Children

In the event you have children with your ex-partner, and if both of you are going to continue to be involved in their lives, some form of communication will have to be maintained as you co-parent.

> Noreen (48): 'Michael and I separated when Niall was six. He saw his dad on Wednesdays and every second weekend. It was not a good separation and we hadn't been getting along for a year before it happened. Eventually his dad moved out. Even though I knew it was the best thing to do, my heart was broken and I missed Michael terribly in the first two years. Niall was also upset at the thought of going to his dad's and I didn't understand at the time that, because we were still not getting on in spite of the separation, the handover times on Wednesdays and at weekends were particularly tense and this was what upset him. It was only when he was a teenager that he admitted he believed that if he didn't have to go to his dad's I wouldn't get so upset. He said he would miss me when I was away and wondered if I was okay because he could see me wiping away my tears at the doorstep.'

As a woman and a mother, it is likely that you are quite familiar with your children's routines, their likes and dislikes, and you may have an intuitive understanding of their needs. In today's world, both men and women have a more prominent role in the nurturing of their children as opposed to it being strictly the mother's domain. Nevertheless, most women will admit that they still feel the greater portion of the nurturing role falls on their shoulders.

When your children are with their dad, it is important that vital elements to their well-being are being maintained by both of you. You can make this clear (if you are the main caregiver) by making a list of your children's routines, likes and dislikes, medication, etc. and giving it to their dad. Whether or not your ex goes with that is up to him and, more often than not, he will do things differently to you. Unfortunately, part of the challenge of co-parenting is learning to accept that there will be differences that may irritate you, but as long as your child is not harmed or neglected, you will have to come to terms with this.

My guess is you'll have enough on your plate without feeling like your ex is pulling against you and making matters worse in terms of parenting or anything else. While you can't control what he says and does, you can make life a lot easier for yourself. He may not be willing to go over old ground about what went wrong. Unfortunately, when dealing with any type of grief, although it might be more normal for a woman to want to communicate, talking about something so emotional is usually a less comfortable place for a man as he finds himself exposed to her pain, especially if he believes he is the cause of it. Sadly, we don't get all the answers, and a lot of them we end up figuring out on our own anyway. In time, hopefully, getting all the answers won't matter.

In Conclusion

Although the path of separation doesn't follow a neat and orderly line, taking care of yourself is paramount to helping you through the journey. There are no rules as to how you should be feeling. Even though you might not be able to see it and may be overwhelmed by your feelings, you do have choices. Some important choices are as follows.

You can choose to:

- accept that it is over and plan for the future

- survive – one day at a time

- learn new skills or polish up on old skills

- seek help

- be there for your children

- not be the victim

- not be lured into fighting

- not be the one who drives an unnecessary legal battle

- recover and rebuild your life

Counselling can help you clarify your thoughts and assist you in developing new strategies. Most women who seek counselling say that they found it helpful and wish they'd done it sooner.

(*Adapted from* 'Women and Separation – Managing New Horizons' by Relationships Australia, http://www.relationships. org.au.)

Chapter 4

Men and Separation

As a woman, I am always interested to hear about men's experiences, both in and out of relationships. In addition, I am also aware that, for a man, entering a counselling room can feel like an unnatural experience; it's the last place they expect to find themselves. More often than not, they enter into counselling with varying degrees of reluctance. It is usually the last thing they will try when they cannot sort things out for themselves. After all, talking about feelings is soft stuff and more suited to women, isn't it?

In an ideal relationship, a man and woman complement each other and will work together as a team. Or so the fairy tale goes, until you start to see your partner's gender qualities as pulling against how you want things to be. Instead of appreciating what your partner brings to the relationship *because* they are male or female, you can see him or her as trying to control or influence you.

Regardless of gender, no two people will experience something the same way. However, a man's experience of separation may be different to that of a woman. I will describe the more common experiences that men face in this chapter.

Men, Feelings and Separation

Like it or not, men are different to women in how they handle emotion. The male and female brain are organised differently, which impacts each sex not only biologically, but psychologically and socially. In all children, brain activity associated with negative emotion is located deep in their brain, in a place called the amygdala. If you compare the brain to an apple, the amydala is located in a similar place to the seeds of an apple. However, during adolescence, the emotional centre in girls shifts to the cerebral cortex, which is closer to the part of the brain where verbal processing and speech happens – similar in location to the skin of an apple. This *only* happens with girls. Hormones aside, this may be why teenage girls are so expressive of their emotions and teenage boys feel very uncomfortable when asked to talk about their feelings. While they are still emotional, they are not expressing it verbally so they may appear to be withdrawn and moody (Sax 2005). This may partly explain why emotions are harder to access for a man than for a woman – men are being asked to connect two parts of their brain that are some distance away from each other and don't communicate on a regular basis.

One of the greatest strengths of a man is that he is more commonly hardwired to be comfortable working from a logical, solution-focused position. In relationships, a man tends to focus on getting to a solution and offers his partner opinions on how to fix a problem that is worrying her, whereas she might not necessarily be looking for an answer, but is more focused on discussing or sharing the problem and her feelings about it. It might be oversimplifying the matter, but perhaps an easy way to look at it is that a masculine approach is to be the 'head' and the feminine approach is to be the 'heart' of a relationship (although the masculine approach isn't always that of the male and visa versa). As mentioned in the last chapter, that's not to say that men can't get emotional and women can't be logical, but there does seem to be a greater natural tendency for each to adopt these roles.

Socially, how a man has been brought up by his family and community and whether, as a boy, he was taught to be 'self-sufficent, self-reliant and independent' (Rando 1991, p. 66) will influence his approach to his feelings. As a boy, a man will have also picked up messages about how to behave emotionally, often suppressing the perceived 'feminine' or softer emotions that would make him vulnerable in a man's world. Even if his mother sat him on her lap in childhood and said, 'There, there, tell me all about it', and he told her all his troubles, this openness will be tempered or dampened down sooner or later. As a boy, he will go out into the world and will have to survive being male, to avoid being seen as the weak one and being picked on by other boys (and sometimes girls). He learns to toughen up and to keep his 'weaker' feelings in control. Fathers often know this instinctively and can be seen by their partners as being hard and unflinching when dealing with their sons. Being a male himself, a father will understand that this is a natural rite of passage for his son, and will try to help him to be strong enough to withstand life's challenges.

The hormone testosterone also plays a role in how a man approaches his feelings. It gives a man drive and aggressive energy; it fuels his sexual libido and helps to make him goal/task-focused, giving him a natural ingredient to mask his emotions. Biologically speaking, testosterone levels drop in men over the age of forty. As he enters middle age, a man becomes more aware of his feelings and softens out. This is one of the effects of ageing and will affect the quality of his relationships going forward. If he has spent all his life being the tough, strong, macho male, it can be a huge challenge as these new, almost uncontrollable feelings take over.

You may have heard that expression 'He never listens and all she wants to do is talk.' It can be deeply frustrating and sometimes overwhelming for a man when he is confronted by his partner to talk about his feelings, which is a lot more normal and natural for her than it is for him. However, a man can go to great emotional depths when he has to. He just does it at a different pace. Unless she understands this, a woman can get impatient waiting. When he doesn't get enough 'space for his pace', a man will give up trying to talk to his partner at all. She is likely to see this as him withdrawing or keeping things from her. In my experience as a relationship counsellor, I often hear women saying at the end of the session, 'I never knew that he felt that way.' What has happened during the hour of counselling is that the man gets room to talk and, once he knows he won't be interrupted, he feels more comfortable about opening up.

Women often have their own well-established support networks, and, even though they are experiencing pain too, they are more likely to be naturally better equipped to deal with it. In the course of researching this book, I've noticed that a lot of self-help books are written for women (and by women). It makes me wonder how isolating this must be for men. How a man deals with the end of a significant relationship will also be influenced by whether he was the one to leave or the one who was left behind. In my professional experience, which is supported by that of many of my colleagues, men are less likely to leave a relationship and go it alone, whereas women are more likely to end a relationship because they are unhappy. That said, whether he was the one to leave or the one who was left behind, a man will still have to deal with some very strong emotions that, at times, can be leave him feeling overwhelmed.

The end of a relationship, although it can be a relief initially, can bring a lot of unhappiness, uncertainty and suffering, even if you were the one to leave. However, men, in most cases, are ill-equipped to deal with 'negative' emotions and can be faced with, at a conscious level anyway, an intense and bewildering mix of feelings that they may not remember having experienced before. This leaves them stunned, confused and not sure what to do next. Separation, for many men, can be one of those times in life when they feel powerless and quite vulnerable. Nobody, even at the best of times, likes to be put in a position where they feel like they have no control.

When Your Partner Leaves You

Some men find themselves in the position of being told that their relationship is over when they didn't even realise that there was a problem in the first place. The reason for this, which may have taken root at a much earlier stage in their relationship, could have been the couple's inability to deal with their differences. The woman may have wanted to be heard and to talk things over, while the man may have wanted to provide the solution, and was instead met with criticism. Both then beat a hasty retreat. Eventually, the woman stopped saying that she was upset about something until one day (and this might have been several years later) she couldn't take it anymore and she told him she was leaving. It would be quite normal for a man in these circumstances to be struck by feelings of shock, disbelief, rage and depression, perhaps leading to suicidal thoughts. He may find it hard to express such painful feelings and feel it 'unmanly' to do so even if he could. This places him in a very vulnerable and powerless position, with a problem he can't solve so he can move on.

When You Leave

Men may not be as sensitive as quickly as women to underlying unhappiness in a relationship. But if he feels unappreciated and unloved over a long period of time, or doubts his own self-worth and confidence, a man will become aware that something is wrong and that he is personally unhappy and lonely. The unfortunate consequence of this is that, rather than going back to his relationship to try to resolve this (maybe he just doesn't know how to), he looks outside the relationship to satisfy him, whether that is becoming more involved with work, with hobbies or with someone else. Men are still statistically twice as likely to have affairs than women.

For some men, the thought of being on their own is unbearable, and, as mentioned, if they feel that their relationship is no longer working for them, they are more likely than women to choose a new partner before leaving the old relationship. Sometimes relationships end when a person (not always a man) has met someone outside the relationship with whom they believe they have a stronger connection. Although these relationships can work out in the long term, very often the emotional problems or patterns of the old relationship will be transferred to the new one and may threaten an individual's new-found happiness, leaving them with a sense of 'Oh no, not again!' Affairs, whether they are emotional, sexual or a combination of both, can be the catalyst for ending a relationship and they can also serve to help a person avoid the pain that comes with separation. Some people jump from one relationship to another all their lives to avoid this pain. Although this is understandable, it can leave them with little wiggle room for personal growth or any real sense of themselves as an individual.

Men and Their Friends

In general, women tend to dictate the flow of emotional communication in a relationship. As the couple become more established, she will tend to make arrangements for them socially with family and friends. Most men are amenable to this when they fall in love, but what it can mean for them is that they take a step away from their own group of friends and family.

So the end of a relationship can be terribly isolating for a man. Will his friends and family welcome him back or ignore him? What if he had few friends before he met his partner – does he now find himself totally on his own if he isn't close to his own family? For a male, when everything is up in the air and the whirlwind of emotions has been unleashed, his confidence can be compromised and he will turn to whomever he can to help sort himself out. He might be putting up a front so his friends and colleagues can't see his pain. The 'I'm OK' mask may be so impenetrable that no one suspects that he's in pain and hurting inside. Even if he does say something, male friends may not be so comfortable with it and may not be able to find the right words to help. Perhaps when they see their friend's struggle and know that there's no clear solution, they find themselves powerless to do anything to change how their friend feels.

Having a few pints with friends will also limit what is said. No one wants anyone to get upset in public, so personal conversation is kept to a minimum. On the other hand, men tend to have more open, straightforward friendships than women. They don't take things so personally and their friendships tend to be less complicated. They don't seem to mind, as women do, if their friends disappear for long stretches. As a man, your buddies are generally happy to see you again when you want to re-join them after perhaps a long period.

Naturally, some friends will be lost along the way. If you are now a single man, some of the friends you had as a result of being in a couple will disappear. However, as you become more settled into your new life, there is now the possibility of new friendships forming with people with whom you may be more compatible as an individual. As you are getting over the end of a relationship and may be single for a while, this is the perfect opportunity to consider the friendships you have or might have had in the past and the qualities that attracted you to those people. They may not necessarily have been intimate relationships, but connections you've had with people that made you feel good – were they just fun to be around, could you debate with each other, go to matches, the pub, etc.?

Understanding what attracts you to other people will help you become more in tune with your own personality and character. And so, when meeting someone new (whether it becomes a friendship or something deeper), you are more likely to put your best foot forward, be your authentic or real self and attract more positive experiences.

Female friends can be enormously helpful at times like this. As women, more often than not they will understand the emotional complexity of what's happening and men can find them soothing company; they can feel understood and talk more freely about their feelings, without running the risk of being seen as weak. If you are in this situation, you may not be able to talk about your worries and concerns with your male friends, and a willing and understanding ear can be very seductive. A female friend can fill the void that your ex may have left. Sometimes, though, what was a platonic friendship can tip into something physical or sexual. In the cold light of day (usually the next morning or shortly afterwards), you might change your mind and just want her back as a friend once again. Yes, it can be comforting to have that kind of closeness in a physical sense, but you take a risk of causing confusion if your female friend has developed feelings for you because you have shared so much with her. Women are not only attracted to strengths in a man, but are also drawn to vulnerability. Crossing the line with a female friend may make her think that you have deeper feelings for her. This will leave her confused if you back away, and it may mean the loss of her friendship.

Regardless of whether they are male or female, a friend who has gone through something similar can be a valuable source of support even if you are not someone who normally talks about your feelings. They will understand much of what you're going through, even if their experience was different.

It is particularly necessary at times like this, when you are most vulnerable, that you have supportive outlets, including friends to whom you can talk about your feelings and pastimes that you enjoy and give you pleasure. If you like dinner parties, you may find yourself being invited to quite a few. Having worked with several groups of men and women over the years who are coming to terms with their separation or divorce, I find that most women feel that single men are a more welcome addition to dinner parties than they are, as single women.

Succumb to the Numb?

As I mentioned earlier, the pain that is experienced at the time of separation can feel like it has come out of nowhere. One day we're alright, and the next it can feel like a bomb has been put under us and our life is lying on the ground in little pieces. As we grapple with what's happened, the danger is that we can become abusive to ourselves by trying to anaesthetise the pain through alcohol, drugs, sex, etc. It's normal not to want to feel pain or, worse, to become vulnerable, which is not a man's natural domain. He will take steps to do whatever he can to overcome these feelings and can often look for the quick-fix answer. However, all drinking and drugging will do is provide short-term relief (and possibly some nasty side effects) that may turn into a long-term problem that could affect your future personal happiness. Damaging numbing behaviour can increase isolation and slows down any emotional healing.

Long-term relationships, for most people, will endure periods of boredom or a sense of 'same thing, different day'. Couples who like to keep their relationships fresh and interesting will change things around and make sure they do enough things they enjoy, both together and separately. When a relationship has been stale for some time, to finally separate can bring relief. There may have been little or no sex, which most men will admit is an important part of a relationship and validates their sense of being loved by their partner. A temporary disappearance of libido is quite normal in the immediate aftermath of separation, but will re-appear as time goes on. During the period after separation, men can find themselves looking for sex without the emotional involvement that is required for a more long-term established relationship. It provides a source of comfort and release and may reassure him of his attractiveness.

However, although casual sex can be exciting in the beginning, for people who are more used to being in a relationship, regardless of whether they are male or female, sex with no emotional depth – and by that I mean the affection and compatibility that comes with sharing your life together – can bring up feelings of emptiness and they may long to fall in love again.

According to Ian McDonald in his book *Men After Separation* (2005, p. 67):

Some men find regular intercourse almost as vital as regular meals. For them there is presumably a remedy in casual sex and I think they probably project their need in a way that finds a response from women with similar needs. Perhaps for many men this sexual regime may be the answer at least in the short term. I am also prepared to believe that it may have more appeal for younger men whose sex drive is at its peak than it would for more mature men who may have sexually slowed down a little. Whatever the answer, I believe that most men in the longer term seek a more fulfilling sex life than 'merely bodies touching'.

It goes without saying that good sexual health includes taking responsibility by using condoms to lower the risk of sexually transmitted infections (STIs).

Men and Counselling

Charlie (56) had been in a relationship with his girlfriend for over 10 years. Over the past three years, she'd talked about wanting to get married. They had both been married before and this was a second relationship, but he was too afraid to commit again. Finally, she left him because she didn't want to wait around any longer, saying that she was getting on and wanted to find someone who was willing to get married. Charlie was heartbroken. Even though he didn't want to get married, he really loved her and didn't want to be with anyone else.

As the weeks went on, he found himself in the pub night after night. His hangovers were getting worse and he found the only way to deal with them was to drop into the pub on the way home from work. On more than one occasion, he found himself beside a stranger when he woke up. He felt terrible because he would have preferred for that woman to have been his ex – he was lonely without her. After a while, he began to get angry and would give out about his ex when anyone would listen. Friends and family were finding him hard to be around and began to keep their distance, which was just making him angrier. Finally, when he was told by his boss to get some help with the drinking, due to absenteeism at work, he realised that he wasn't coping at all. He now felt ashamed and guilty, on top of all the other horrible feelings.

Faced with what he thought was lying ahead of him if he didn't sort himself out, he did go and see a counsellor. Initially he felt it was no different to talking to someone in the pub, but at least she was listening to him and she did seem to understand his confusion. She didn't judge him or tell him what to do, although this is what he really wanted, for someone else to take control, because at that point he felt like he was losing his mind.

Slowly he began to trust her. Even when he was most confused and troubled, she stayed in there with him, gently encouraging him to keep going. Although he wasn't sure what was happening in counselling a lot of the time, he did notice that he was able to concentrate better at work. He still went to the pub regularly but he didn't drink as much and began to play football again. He would say that because he was able to speak his mind to the counsellor and leave what he had said in her office, he felt better overall. When he went out socially, he was in better humour and felt more like his old self. As the worst of the pain and confusion passed, he then began to look at his own fears about commitment.

Just a word here about getting professional help, such as counselling: although going to see a counsellor is more common-place nowadays, some people will see it as an admission of failure, that is, that they couldn't sort out their problems themselves. In reality, people use therapy for lots of different reasons but, ultimately, their goal is to figure out the best way forward for them. Yes, it takes courage to talk to a stranger and place your trust in them when you are struggling – a good counsellor knows this and will be respectful of their client's situation.

The purpose of counselling during separation is to help clients grieve healthily and to take back control of their lives. From my own experience as a practitioner, clients are likely to come back from time to time for a short period when something is troubling them, because they know from previous experiences that it can be quite empowering. If you have never used counselling before but feel that you might like to try it, why not say that to a counsellor and see how you get on, without committing yourself to more than one meeting?

Communicating with Your Ex

Staying in touch with your ex is unavoidable if you have shared assets or children. You are no longer a couple, yet there is a practical need to stay in touch and very few people can afford to continuously go through their solicitors.

Women like to talk to clear the air and can appear emotional to a man when doing so. They are expressive in their facial gestures, their body language and their tone of voice, to which men are very sensitive. Some men can feel quite threatened by this, especially if they are not used to talking about their own feelings.

Physiologically, when a man feels under threat his heart rate will rise; he can feel overwhelmed and can react by either stonewalling ('disappearing', either literally by leaving the room or by distracting himself with other things, like flicking the remote control, looking all around him but not at his ex, or hiding behind the newspaper, Xbox, PSP, etc.) or becoming defensive himself by getting angry, contemptuous or critical of his ex. Whatever way he reacts, his objective is to put some distance between them both so he can calm down and gain control of his emotions once again.

It can be helpful to be able to communicate to your ex-partner that you might need time out in conflict situations to sort things out in your head. Be clear on how long you need (half an hour, an hour or longer) and make sure you do come back to the issue in hand as quickly as you can. If you are doing it to avoid having the conversation, she will be sensitive to that and will be reluctant to trust your words. If you say you'll do something and then you back out of it, this tells her that you are unreliable. If at all possible, another option is to take a few deep breaths to steady yourself and get your heartbeat back to normal so you can continue the conversation without any time out.

Please be aware, too, that there are probably some very strong residual feelings there between you and that you both are probably feeling quite defensive, a situation that may go on for quite some time. If you are a man who has left the family home as a result of your partner wanting to separate, you may feel like you have lost everything, which naturally would seem unfair and unjust to you.

A typical conversation between a couple who have just broken up can go as follows:

Her: Why haven't you called me to sort out your stuff? The problem with you is that you always leave everything to me. [*This can sound like criticism.*]

Him: That's it – blame me for everything as usual! [*Feeling blamed and now defensive.*]

Her: I asked you two weeks ago to move your stuff. Honestly, can you blame me for being mad at you? Your stuff is taking up room and should be gone by now. [*Feeling defensive and justifying position.*]

Him: Whatever. I just can't win with you can I? Everything I do is wrong!

If a man can take one step back, he will automatically be more in control. When a person feels criticised, they will naturally want to defend themselves. Criticism from a woman is usually her response to being hurt or ignored in some way. She will tend to use a lot of words to communicate her meaning, and will use hyperbole to get her point across through using words such as 'always' and 'never' (Gray, 1993) – this is a signal that she is hurt. The most important thing you can do for yourself (and I know it's hard to be generous when you're in a bad place) is to empathise with her feelings, rather than what she's just said. Ironically, you are not backing down; you are taking control of the situation by not letting her overwhelm you. She might speak for another few minutes but she *will* calm down, and so will you, especially if you remain in control.

Although there are no guarantees, a more productive conversation for both people would go something like this:

Her: Why haven't you called me to sort out your stuff? The problem with you is that you always leave everything to me. [*This can sound like criticism.*]

[*The time for a deep breath is right about now!*]

Him: I'm sorry if you're annoyed. I've just been busy with other things. This has been a big change for me too. [*Acknowledging her feelings (empathy) and stating his own side calmly.*]

Her: I asked you two weeks ago to move the stuff and I just thought it would be done by now. I know it's a big change for us but we do need to be moving on with our lives. [*Less critical and more acknowledging of both positions.*]

[*Another deep breath here.*]

Him: So what do I need to move? [*Taking charge and being less defensive. Looking for specifics so he knows what to do next.*]

Her: I have it all packed up and ready to go. When can you come and collect it? [*She's being specific and letting him decide, rather than 'ordering' him around.*]

One of the key things the man in this situation has done here is to admit his own feelings by saying that he's trying to adjust to the change, rather than coming across to her like he doesn't care. By acknowledging her feelings as well, she is more likely to calm down because he has shown that he understands her position. Now both are more likely to resolve the issue. Don't give up this approach if it doesn't work the first or second time. The reason why I say this is that you and your ex-partner may have been used to communicating differently. It is similar to writing with one hand when you are used to using the other.

Men and their Children

If you have been in a long-term relationship but do not have children or joint assets and liabilities breaking up is usually more straightforward. This is not to underestimate the heartbreak involved, but if you leave a relationship taking more or less what you brought with you into the relationship then the break is cleaner.

However, the longer you are with someone, the more likely it is that you accumulate things jointly. If this is the case, with breaking up comes the complex process of how you will divide your possessions in a way that is fair to both. If the relationship was one in which the couple assumed traditional roles of financial provider and homemaker, regardless of whether there are children or not, this can further complicate things when deciding who is entitled to what in terms of possessions.

Usually, up until now anyway, it is the man who leaves the family home when a couple separates. If children are involved, many men will express their concern about not being there enough for their children and will want to see them as often as possible. One of their biggest fears is losing contact with them altogether. Any perceived 'obstacles' to seeing the children will only intensify this fear. Children are naturally upset when their dad is gone from the family home and he may be at a loss to know how to respond to his children's pain, if his ex-partner was the one who did the calming down and the drying away of tears when they were all together as a family.

In addition, they now have to consider where they're going to live and how they're going to afford it all. Many men tend to take the cheapest option for obvious reasons. While they may see it as a short-term solution, in reality they may be in this accommodation for quite a while longer than anticipated. Many find themselves having to contend with damp, cold, depressing accommodation or impinging on others' generosity and space. It doesn't take Einstein to figure out that this will not help matters in the long run. Also, it's worth considering if there is adequate room to accommodate children when they come to visit. Many men who have substandard accommodation, or are being accommodated by friends or family in terms of living space, find they have nowhere to bring their children and the only options for them is somewhere like McDonald's, parks, museums, the cinema, etc. This also compounds a feeling of inadequacy. And to make matters worse, their ex may have a tendency to see that Daddy gets all the fun things to do, while they're left with the humdrum routines.

However, in some cases, men may be left literally 'holding the baby'. Nowadays, some couples decide for practical reasons that the woman is the sole breadwinner and, when a break-up ensues, the stay-at-home dad may be in the precarious position of maintaining his role as the principal care-giver as well as having to return to work in order to pay the bills. He is naturally concerned about wanting to provide for his family and is worried (as is his ex-partner) about whether there will be enough for all, especially for his children.

In Conclusion

There are some newly separated men who are at a loss as to how to manage daily life. They may not be as adept as women at housework or nutrition, especially if they have played a more traditional role in the family. Not taking good care of themselves will slow down their ability to deal with what has happened, as poor nutrition affects a person psychologically as well as physically. Although the impact of separation is not necessarily age specific, older men can become very lonely. They may be reluctant to start any new relationship. As with Charlie, in the case study above, rather than making a new life for himself, a man can gravitate towards alcohol for relief. With a deteriorating social life, substance abuse increases and soon damages his health. Research and greater suicide rates among young males tell us that men are more vulnerable to suicide as a permanent solution to what they do not realise is a temporary problem. Is it possible that they do not know how to ask for help or where to go?

A bad relationship can have a lasting impact on an individual and meeting someone new can be nerve-racking, especially if you have been off the dating scene for quite a long time. Underpinning this is an anxiety about repeating mistakes made in the past; trusting someone again and entering a new relationship seems a bit risky. After all, if it doesn't work out, you will have to go through all that pain again and might question if any relationship is worth it.

There are no guarantees that any relationship will last, but if you are hopeful of starting again with someone new, take your time and don't rush into the first relationship that comes your way. Wait until you are feeling happier in yourself again and you might find that you are more relaxed and content in spite of what has happened, which will make you all the more attractive to a new partner.

Chapter 5

Co-Parenting

Telling the Children

Imagine visiting a country where you do not speak the language. You are about to embark on a train journey, have purchased your ticket and are about to board when an alarm goes off. You wonder what's happened. 'Am I in danger?' you ask yourself. 'Or it is something minor and nothing to worry about?' You look around to see what's happening and everyone is talking at once. You sense panic and distress, and people begin moving quickly in different directions. You ask the nearest person what's happening, but because they speak a different language they're not making any sense. You're not quite sure what's going on, but clearly it's not good news. No one is taking control and now you begin to panic.

This is what a child's experience can be like when they are told that their parents are separating. It is really important to plan and consider carefully how your child is informed of your separation. Children are like sponges – they take in the emotions around them without understanding what they are about. They will feel your distress, see your upset, but not really understand everything that's being said. A parent is usually the first person a child will turn to for reassurance when they are anxious. If you, as the parent, are panicked and not in control consider what affect this will have on your child.

The moment a child hears the news that their parents are separating becomes one that they will recall, even years later, in great detail: 'It was a Wednesday and we were in the kitchen – I remember because it was the week before we were going on holidays.' How they are told and the manner in which the news is relayed will have an impact on children. It might seem obvious, but take care how you do it and what you say.

When children notice that their parents aren't getting on, they may ask the question, 'Are you going to separate?' Nowadays, it is unusual for a child not to have at least one friend or classmate whose parents have split up. However, it goes without saying that it is not a good idea to blurt out anything about separating unless the decision is final. Conversely, in some families, even though the decision has been made it can be weeks or sometimes months before the children will be told, even if one parent has already left the family home. The children may be too afraid to ask what is going on – they know there is something wrong but don't want to add further upset. Stress or anxiety that cannot be expressed can manifest itself as changed behaviour at home or at school.

In an ideal world, both parents would gather the family together and deliver the information simply and without blame, informing the children what will happen next. It takes courage, maturity and control for parents to deliver this kind of information to their children. Knowing ahead of time what you want to say is terribly important. It is quite natural to want to defend your own point of view. Parents will not want to be seen as the cause of their children being caught in the middle of what is going on between them as a couple. Neither will they want to be seen as the 'baddie'. However, they will want their children to support their decision. When they see their children upset, sad or angry at what has happened, it can have an effect on them as the parent. They will possibly feel guilty or want to blame the other parent – 'You're going to have to get used to this – I didn't want this to happen either but your mother/father doesn't want us to be together anymore'; or 'We couldn't stay together anymore because your mother/father doesn't love me/us.' Children who are not yet adults will not understand what romantic love is and that not being 'in love' anymore doesn't necessarily mean that their mum and dad hate each other.

It is unreasonable to expect your children to agree with or support the decision to separate – even if that is what you want, and there is unhappiness in the home, children are more likely to want their parents to stay together than to part. On the other hand, in some families where parents have been arguing a lot children can feel temporarily relieved when a separation finally happens because, for them, it means that there will be no more fighting in the family home.

So, what do you tell your children and how can you do it in a way that prioritises their needs? It is, after all, upsetting news and yet you will want them to be able to take it in with minimal upset. The best way can often be the simplest. If you and your ex-partner are telling your children together, try to agree on who will say what. Please bear in mind that using the word 'we' takes the blame out of the situation – 'We haven't been getting on and have made the decision to separate. But we want you to know that we both love you and will do our best to help you get through this.'

When you first talk with your children, keep the discussion to the most important and most immediate issues; too much information will be confusing. Children need to hear that their basic needs will be met, that someone will still fix breakfast in the morning, help them with their homework and tuck them into bed at night. Children also need to know that their relationship with *both* parents will continue, if possible. Try to talk to them in a reasonably limited time frame – children have a limited attention span anyway, but when explanations drag on and on they can become confused. You, as the parents, may depart from the plan of what you meant to say, thereby increasing the risk of needless upset. Later on, children may become more curious and start asking questions, but, initially, keep to the point as best you can. Afterwards, you can figure out some of the answers to their questions but try to keep your partner's and your own integrity intact, even if you feel inclined to say negative things about your partner. It will not help and your child may start avoiding any conversation on the topic altogether as a result.

Please be aware that everyone grieves differently and while one child might be feeling sad and clingy, another will be feeling like they need a bit of space because they are so upset. Even though it's a difficult time for you, your children still need you to take care of them and they will look to you for reassurance (this may also include assurance that they are not to blame for the separation). When they have been told the news, check in with them shortly afterwards and see how they're doing. They may be confused and upset or just plain numb and not able to make sense of what's happening. You may not be able to make much sense of what they are saying either, so try to stay calm and reassuring for them. If they want to talk, they will want you to hear them, *really hear them*, and acknowledge their feelings, so you might respond by saying, 'I know you're very sad and I'm very sorry this has happened to our family.' This gives them a sense that they are understood and can be a helpful way for them to deal with their own distress. Younger children are more likely to tell you how they are feeling than older ones. If a child is quiet, do not make the assumption that they are okay. It will never be a waste of time to check in with them.

Children may not want to overburden you, especially if they know that you are upset. If you are aware of an adult with whom they get on well, please ask them to keep an eye on and make special time for your children. This will help them avoid bottling up their own grief. It is quite normal at this time for them to find it difficult to concentrate at school and it is important that teachers are made aware of the situation at home.

Age-Related Reactions

Although it is their parents who are separating, children are deeply emotionally involved and it is nearly impossible for them to remain untouched by their parents' pain as well as having to deal with their own grief. There are many sources available on the different reactions children have to separation, depending on their age. I have detailed below the more common experiences and how parents can help their children to adjust in each situation.

Infants

Even infants will notice something is happening. They are extremely sensitive to your emotions. They may become more fretful and easily irritable at this time, and may find it difficult to settle into their normal routines, such as nap times, etc.

As their parents, it's important for you to keep routines as normal as possible. As with all children, infants will find your presence comforting, as well as hugs and soft words. In addition, favourite toys, blankets, etc. can be soothing to them when they're upset.

Toddlers

Toddlers will know when one parent is no longer in the home and will also be sensitive to the emotional atmosphere. It is quite common to see them comforting a parent who is upset. They may also become quite angry with parents and may regress into more baby-like behaviours, for example, thumb-sucking and loss of toilet-training skills that have been recently developed. Toddlers' routines may also become disrupted. They may not sleep as well and can be more prone to nightmares.

What they need is for you to spend more time with them before you leave them, for example, if they're going to a crèche or baby minders, just hang on a few more minutes to make sure they're settled in. Even at this young age, they do need reassurance that they are loved by you. Stay calm if you notice they are regressing to more babyish behaviour – it will disappear over time as they adjust to what has happened. Make sure that other people in their lives know what's going on so that they can provide additional support to a child when they need it.

Pre-School and Early School-Going Children

This age group will usually recognise that they are now living with just one parent. They should have a good understanding that separation means their parents are no longer living together and that they are no longer in love with each other.

They may blame themselves for the separation and worry about the future. This anxiety can come out in nightmares. The child may also be very expressive of their sadness because of the separation. They may also blame one of the parents and become very angry and possibly aggressive towards them. One of the big challenges at this age is to become aware of the difference between fantasy and reality, and the child may fantasise about their parents getting back together.

They need reassurance from you that they are not to blame for the separation, and clarity on matters such as who will be taking care of them and what is happening next. Keep it simple. Be sensitive to their fears. Even if they are angry with you, take a deep breath and acknowledge their feelings without becoming defensive yourself. Be supportive of your children's ongoing need to be with the other parent. Schedule in time so that this can happen. Because they tend to fantasise about their parents getting back together again (and this can happen at any age really), gently but firmly inform them that the separation is final and that you will not be getting back with their other parent.

Pre-Teens and Adolescents

Even though they are older, this age group may also have difficulty accepting the reality of the changes due to the separation of their parents. Not discounting the distress of other children, those in this age group are often the ones most deeply affected. Although they are becoming more independent of you both, they will still expect you to act like a rock while they develop into young adulthood. Like their younger counterparts, they may blame themselves for the separation and yet feel abandoned by the parent who has left. Children of this age group may withdraw from you, their friends and even favourite activities. They can act out how they're feeling and be angry and uncertain about their beliefs concerning love, marriage and family.

Some children feel they grow up too soon and may develop a heightened sense of responsibility, worrying about things like there not being enough money. They may have had to assume new roles within the family and this further compounds the loss they've experienced.

They do need reassurance from you that they are loved. If at all possible, both parents should keep an active interest in their children's lives, friends, schoolwork, etc. Keep communication lines open with children from this age group and keep to the family routines and rituals as much as you can. Even though they are older, they do need regularity during what is an unsettling time.

If their household responsibilities have to increase, try to make the tasks age appropriate and show appreciation when they have completed their tasks.

Even though they may be quite mature, no child (regardless of age) should be expected to be their parent(s)' confidante.

In her book *When Parents Split* (2008, pp. 1–2), Glynis Good recounts the experiences of adolescents during and after parental separation in order to highlight the unique difficulties they face:

> Sarah (17): 'My parents were always fighting and shouting and then they wouldn't talk to each other for days. It was just normal in our house. Afterwards, I wasn't really surprised that they separated but I still don't think I was prepared for it. I don't think anyone ever really is.'

Mark (12): 'I always thought my parents were happy and got on. We never saw anything that would have hinted that they weren't. I never saw it coming. I still can't believe that they have separated. I had no idea. It was like one day we were a happy family and the next day they were telling us we weren't. I never thought it would happen to my parents.'

The Differing Needs of Adults and Children During Separation and Divorce

We may think children's needs remain constant, but they do change during separation. The intense feelings that are a response to the huge loss that a family experiences at this time are common to both adults and children. Adults may yearn for space from their partner, but children will want to remain close to both their parents. As mentioned, children will often fantasise about their parents getting back together, even if one or both of them enters a new relationship and even re-marries. Even though a separation may mean an end to arguing or tension, children will prefer that their parents stay together despite the unhappiness.

Children need more, not less, information about what is happening. However, parents may be tempted to avoid talking about it. Children will pick up on their parents' avoidance and treat it as a 'no-go' area. Their imaginations are fertile and they might start believing that when they aren't being told something, it is because it is something really bad.

Routines are very important to children, especially when they are experiencing change. However, as an adult, it can be difficult and seem impossible to keep to a routine when you're so upset. Try to keep to the same routines for meal times, bedtimes and so on. Believe it or not, and difficult as it might be to do, routine will help everyone in the home.

Most adults need time to take stock of their lives during and after separation before they can decide what to do next.

Children, on the other hand, prefer to know, sooner rather than later, what they can expect.

It can be difficult to hear that your child is upset or angry with you, and yet they do need to be able to express their painful emotions. For children, when a parent leaves, they may feel that it's because the parent doesn't love them as opposed to because the adult relationship has ended – after all, Dad/Mum wouldn't leave them if they loved them, would they? Children aren't interested in the finer details of the reasons for separation but will want to know that they are not to blame. They do need constant reassurance that they are loved by both parents and that they are free to love them both without having to take sides.

Allow your children time to adjust to the new situation (especially before a new partner is introduced). You may have known about the separation and change for a significantly longer time, and they just need to be given a chance to catch up and to establish an after-separation relationship with both of you.

Ongoing Parenting

In the time between the decision to separate and when one or both of you have settled into your new home(s), you will continue to be a mother and father to your children. What has changed are your circumstances and with that comes the negotiation of new arrangements so that children have access to both of you. Continuing to act out your couple issues as time goes on means that your children will ultimately suffer.

A parenting plan will provide continuity for your children in their relationship with each parent and can be agreed either between yourselves or with a professional. The purpose of it is to make it clear to all how time is shared out between parents, where the children will stay (although this will be more uncertain in the beginning unless two homes are available), pick-up and drop-off arrangements, how regular contact is maintained between the children and both their parents, how responsibilities are managed between the parents, and how decisions about school arrangements, child care, holidays, pocket money, etc. are made. In essence, a good parenting plan takes into account everyone's needs and interests most of the time. Some parents end up living long distances away from each other and, as a result, the children may not see the absent parent as much. If you live far away, try to make sure that you are in regular contact with your children. If you have the children most of the time, provide some mode of access to the other parent, whether it is by landline, mobile phone, Skype, etc.

The benefit of having an agreed plan for children is that they know what is happening – when parents communicate constructively they avoid the difficulties children experience when they feel caught between two parents whom they love. It is recommended that you consult your children about their concerns, but they should never be made to feel under pressure to make a decision – that is your role as their parents.

Although it can be easier and more convenient to convey messages to each other through the children, it does unfortunately place an added burden on young shoulders, especially when they look to you as the adults to sort this out between you and keep them out of it. Children will often take on the role of messenger in the hope that their parents will start talking again and relieve them of the chore; instead, they become privy to the painful nuances of adult separation and they become the gatekeepers of communication between their parents, when all they want to do is get on with growing up.

Conor (16): 'I used to see myself as a bridge between my parents ... a bit like a rope bridge linking two very steep rocky sides with a huge drop below ... I got it wrong. They never managed to really talk to each other properly again. Me running back and forwards across it was useless. I was the only one on it. In the end I just got on with trying to have as good a relationship as I could with them individually, and left them to get on with whatever communication or non-communication they decided for themselves.' (Good 2008, p. 26)

A parenting plan also has benefits for adults because it helps them to communicate the nuts and bolts of parenting in a different way. When a couple are in a relationship together and then go on to have a baby, their roles in terms of the care of that child are often unspoken. They must now learn to be more clear or explicit about how they wish to parent their children as a separated couple – 'You look after this and I look after that.' If you are the parent who is more used to minding the children, you are probably familiar with their likes and dislikes as well as their habits and routines. Make this part of the parenting plan so the other parent knows what to anticipate. For both parents, a parenting plan provides a map or a template for negotiating the way forward in terms of parenting.

Parenting is such a primitive and often instinctual role that one of the most common difficulties that appears after separation is how the other parent is 'doing their job'. This is underpinned by the loss of control that you have over your children while they are at their other parent's home and can be further compounded if there is a new partner on the scene. Yes, it is quite natural for you as parents to have different parenting styles – in fact, you can expect to have differences – however, your ex-partner is just as much a parent as you are. In the beginning anyway, you may want to know every detail of how your child was when they were away from you. Of course you will worry that they are okay but it will require a level of trust in your ex-partner. You may have to conceal your disapproval if the other parent doesn't do things exactly the way you would yourself. Children may also behave differently with their other parent. This can have something to do with how custody and access are arranged. Where the children live most of the time is normally where they'll feel most secure – 'I trust this parent so I feel safe to test him/her.' The parent who left is not normally viewed as being as reliable – 'They've already left once and they might leave my life for good, so I'd better not push it.' That is often why the tears and tantrums are more commonly displayed in front of the custodial parent, while children are quite well behaved with the non-custodial parent.

A word on parenting plans: they are only plans and not set in stone. It is up to each parent to see how it goes and how well the children are settling, what works, what doesn't and to renegotiate as necessary. As children become adolescents, a normal part of their own development is that they want to spend more time with their own friends and be more independent of you both. This can be hard on the non-custodial parent, who gets to see them for only a limited period anyway. Another point to consider for the custodial parent is that events and invitations that are due to take place when your ex has the children need to be passed on (and not organised by you without consultation or agreement with the other parent). If everything is set up by the custodial parent, the non-custodial parent can feel they don't have any control of or say in their children's lives, even when the children are in their care. Even though you might feel you know what is best for your children, it is not your decision what they do when they are away from you and with their other parent.

Parents of Adult Children

The impact of parental separation on adult children can often go unnoticed. They are expected to be able to handle it because they are adults and yet they are often more likely to get drawn into their parents' issues. Even when a person has a strong sense of their own identity, separate to that of the family, this can be a time when any boundaries between you and your children can disappear as you feel quite helpless and uncertain about the future. Because they are adults, you might feel they will understand you, and you involve them in order to get the support you need as you get back on your feet. What you say to them is often what you should be saying to your ex, and they get drawn into your grief as well as their own.

Mary (28) was distraught to find out that her parents' marriage was ending. Initially, she took the news calmly because she knew that they hadn't been getting on for several years. However, over the months she became more unsettled as her parents were adjusting to their new lives without each other. She and her mother became more like friends than mother and daughter as so much of their conversation was about the separation. Mary started to feel quite low and, although she had been in a relationship herself for about a year, she began to question whether relationships were meant to last. She realised she wasn't as happy or as carefree as she had been up to this point. She didn't feel her background was that stable anymore and wondered if she herself was stable. Her view of herself was changing.

Her mother seemed to want more of her time as well and she felt responsible for helping her to pick up the pieces. If she had pulled back and tried to stay out of it, she was afraid her mother would feel like she was abandoning her too.

On top of all this, Mary started to look at her father differently. He was the one who announced that he was leaving her mother and she discovered from her mother that it was because he had met someone else. She was angry because she felt that, not only had he left her mother, but he had also betrayed her.

Continued bitterness and anger towards your ex-partner can affect your children far more deeply than the separation itself.

Part-Time Parenting

Just because you do not have the children full time, this does not mean that you have any less of a role to play in terms of parenting. The other parent will bear the brunt of the every-day management of the children. This is often the non-fun role and, as a single parent, this may well be tougher for them than when you were together. However, for you as the non-custodial parent, you can feel lonely and yearn for your children, and you can have a sense of isolation from the family – clearly a loss for both of you. You may see your loss as bigger and more significant than your partner's. In reality, this is rarely the case – there are no winners. However, if you are going to parent as a separated or divorced person, how you do it will help the entire family come to terms with the loss. So here are few tips that can make it easier for you and for everyone else in the family.

Think of co-parenting like a relay race – everyone has their part to play and crucial to a successful team are the moments leading up to and including handing over the baton. The baton symbolises the handover of the parenting responsibility. This takes practice – sometimes the baton will fall, causing frustration for everyone, but it only takes someone to say, 'Let's try to see how we can avoid it happening again' to improve things. Consider yourselves as the athletes. Even if you don't like the other athlete, you will have to talk to them about the baton and what you're going to do with it. Your cooperation is needed, even if you want to keep the baton all to yourself and keep running with it. The other athlete will have to take the baton from you at some point, so do you want a smooth handover or an awkward one? Civility is very important, especially when there are still unresolved issues between you.

You will be keen that your children are happy when they are with you and you will want to tell them what you have in mind to do when they are with you. It is a good idea to discuss these plans with your ex before finalising them with the children. I know you might feel it's none of their business, but doing this shows respect for your ex *as the children's other parent*, regardless of how you feel about them personally. More to the point is that you'll be showing your children that their parents are in control of matters regarding their welfare and that they can still work together as parents, even if they are no longer a couple. Conferring with your ex-partner is very important, especially in the early days when a lot of arrangements are still up in the air and yet to be settled.

Outlined below are some tips for part-time parents to help them and their ex-partners to make things positive for everyone involved. These have been reproduced from *Parenting After Separation: Making the Most of Family Changes* by Jill Burrett (2002, pp. 89–90). Please bear in mind that these points were written based on the assumption that the father is the part-time parent.

- Try to communicate amicably about everything to do with seeing the children, even if you feel that you are always having to compromise. It's worth it! This probably sounds obvious, but it is surprising how often parents fail to do this. Remember, even a controlled iciness towards one another in front of the children is unpleasant for them, so it's more than just avoiding disagreements in their presence that's required, it's being cheery.

- You will be anxious to do everything to help the children feel positive about seeing you, and so naturally you will want to take into account their opinions about the timing of their contact with you. They will probably want to please you and will be reassured by being able to make arrangements with you, but it is usually best to make plans with Mum before you can safely regard them as definite. This especially applies in the early period after separation when everyone is only just getting used to the new routine and misunderstandings are common. The children will be reassured that you and Mum can still cooperate about them. And team responsibility certainly won't work without consultation.

- You may risk the children feeling that they have to make awkward choices between two loved ones if you give them too much say about their arrangements. You and Mum need to be in charge of the organising and decisions, not them, at least not to begin with, and for some time if things remain a bit strained between you. But make sure that you listen to their opinions.

- Stick to arrangements which you have made so that the children don't get disappointed, and your ex does not get irritated. A bit of give and take is good too, as even the best laid plans have to be changed sometimes. In other words, don't change things for no reason, and never forget to let her know. Obvious? Yes, but often forgotten, and a source of great annoyance. If you sometimes resent having to be quite so answerable to her, just remind yourself of the position the children might be put in. For example, if she cuts short her Sunday outing to be home when you said you would be back with the children, and you don't turn up for another two hours, she will be annoyed. And the children will sense this, which puts them in an awkward position in relation to their parents, who seem to be competing for time with them, and who both seem impossible to please! It's just the sort of scenario that you want to avoid, as it can leave a nasty feeling associated with the handover from Dad to Mum. A phone call from you to warn her that you'll be late will more than likely prevent this happening.

- If the children don't come when you are expecting them, don't be too ready to think that Mum isn't sticking to the arrangements. Sometime it really is quite hard to fit everything that has to be done into the week and to put the right priority on things. However, a phone call from your ex to advise why this is so would be a reasonable response to expect, and you should express to her your disappointment and concern. Try to be patient and accepting until you can get together and talk about the problem. A trusted mutual friend can often help with such discussions if they look like being a bit delicate.

- Unless you have worked out a system for belongings, make sure that the clothes and possessions the children come with, when they are staying over, are taken back to Mum's place. A list inside their bag so that you can check it with them when preparing to leave is a help, not an insult to your intelligence, or an attempt to control you! This simple solution will avoid any resentment about mislaid or forgotten possessions – she's probably right, you won't remember everything you should be sending back with them. (Unfortunately, many men are quite inexperienced with clothing, laundry and other domestic matters, and give the impression that they think they are unimportant. This can lead to ill feeling.) If your ex is easy-going and unconcerned about this sort of thing, all well and good. Even so, if you have time, sort what is dirty and what is clean. She won't always be able to guess this, and you will save her a lot of work. Your efforts will be appreciated.

• It's a good idea to have things for them that belong at your place – things they enjoy only when they are with you. This will give them an extra sense of belonging there. Invest in some spare clothes that stay with you too. Aim to make the whole situation simple and hassle free for the children. You'll find this easier if you are fortunate enough to have reasonably homely surroundings yourself, or if you are living with relations. But children can cope with accommodation limitations better than you may imagine.

• Even though family times like Christmas are particularly hard without the children you so much want to be with, try to see the situation from their point of view. If they are having a great time, and none of the grown-ups are feeling bitter and resentful about the arrangements, then all will be well, and you must find yourself a constructive alternative to spending Christmas alone. Do something really different or unusual on Christmas Day so that you don't dwell on the children too much. Try to be flexible about seeing them on special days, unless there is an easy way of arranging it which suits everybody. There aren't enough days in a week for children (especially school-aged ones) to share between two households, two sets of friends and lots of relations. They are usually just as happy having two celebrations at different times, instead of one, unless someone has made them think that the real day is terribly important. Whoever heard of a child who would happily have one party when they could have two?

- Consider the idea, if it appeals to you, of having the children for an extended period in their school holidays, when they seem ready for this. You'll find that it gives you all better opportunities to become really close and to share more of the ordinary experiences which you normally miss out on. Weekends can be a bit of a rush. It is best to discuss any new arrangements with Mum first, as we have already mentioned, so as not to raise false hopes. There may be valid reasons why it might not be a good idea. There is no reason to feel that you must have leave from work just because you're having an extended visit from your children, although it may well be more enjoyable if you do. Depending on your present family circumstances, your relations' desire to spend some time with your children, the extent to which you can enjoyably involve them in your work, the flexibility of your hours, and so on, you may well be able to meet most of your work commitments while your children are with you.

- Getting on with some of what you have to do may give the children a much more normal and realistic experience of life with you, one they can really feel part of. You can't always drop everything to attend to your children when they come to your place and, in any case, it may not be as beneficial to them to have only a 'holiday relationship' with you. A happy medium is best; although it is important that they feel you do have lots of time for them and don't seem too preoccupied with activities that don't concern them directly, especially at the beginning. If you're always surrounded by friends, doing grown-up things, and they have to tag along, they may come to feel that they're not important enough to you and may become less interested in seeing you. Children need some one-on-one time to feel valued by you.

(Reproduced with the publisher's permission from Jill Burrett (2002), *Parenting After Separation: Making the Most of Family Changes*, Sydney, Australia: Finch Publishing.)

Conclusion

Changing the way you parent together is an awkward hurdle at best and is made even more difficult if things aren't easy between you both. There may be less money than before and you may have less or more free time than when you were together. Your current living conditions may not be ideal for children either. You will need to learn how to co-parent because it is critical to the well-being of your family following separation. You are still a family, even if you are no longer together. Be positive, helpful and supportive of the other parent, and seek outside help if you don't feel confident enough to negotiate matters between you. If you follow as many as possible of the guidelines below for parenting as a separated couple, it'll make the transition a much easier one for the entire family in the long run.

Guidelines for co-parenting:

- Be flexible.

- Cooperate with the other parent and have the children ready on time for the handover.

- Be consistent. Do what you say you'll do in relation to time-keeping, responsibilities and tasks – why upset the applecart needlessly? If plans need to be changed, which they sometimes do, give the other parent as much notice as possible.

- Keep any differences you have as a former couple away from little ears.

- Avoid questioning the children about the other parent. You may want to find out about what's going on in their lives, but it is none of your business anymore and it puts your children under pressure to take sides – not fair!

- Do not allow the children to have too much power or they will play you off against each other. This has a nasty tendency to prolong any tension that may be still there between the two of you.

- Try to be decent with your ex-partner (even if they cheated on you or you perceive the separation as their fault) when it comes to the children. When a separation happens, everyone will lose – you, your ex, your children and the extended family. Do your best to come together and work it out for their benefit – do what is truly best for your kids, not what you feel is fair to you and your ex.

Finally, the following is worth remembering:

- Studies show that a close relationship with both parents most helps the adjustment of the children after separation.

- It is not possible to avoid the pain that separation brings to each child, but with care and working together as two parents you can avoid a lot of the damage.

- Never underestimate the importance and value of your relationship with your children, regardless of your circumstances.

- Be proactive in getting support for managing your own stress. Do not rely on your children for this.

- Normal adolescence will bring parenting challenges. Be discerning in distinguishing everyday adolescent issues from issues relating to family separation. Not all problems will have to do with your separation.

- You will always be your child's parent and so will their other parent. Endeavour to work together in a constructive way on parenting issues and put other issues to one side for these times.

- In step or second families, young people can sometimes adjust better and more willingly than the adults involved. Be careful that your own negative feelings towards your children's involvement in this extended family do not hinder their adjustment.

- Remember, as your children get older the same access and visitation arrangements you have had previously may no longer work for them as their school and social lives change. Talk to them and together find a way to make new arrangements that will work to fit their life and yours.

- The faith you have in your child will help them to have faith in themselves.

- Your relationship with your child will hugely influence their life – make it a positive one.

Chapter 6

Living Together When It's Over

Very few couples physically leave each other the moment the decision to separate has been made. This chapter explores what can happen in the home until such time as one or both people can move out and is focused on dealing with that interim or waiting period.

During recessionary times, many separating couples are forced to stay in the same home for longer than may have been the case in the boom times because, financially, they have no other option. A couple might agree that they will separate in the short or medium future, but they may have to wait for a while until it becomes possible. This is quite a different situation from two individuals continuing to live in the same house because they believe that their children would do better with both parents living together; or because they have been together so long they wouldn't know how to be without each other even if they now live parallel lives and are no longer close. They may feel that marriage is for life and leaving is not an option. They might hope that, even if they haven't been close for a long time, things might change between them in the future.

Any person who finds themselves in the position where they feel they have to stay together, regardless of the reason, will identify with the pressure of having to share their home with their partner when their couple relationship has ended.

Staying Together When the Love Is Gone

Mark (52) was married to Angela (50) for thirty years until she decided that she wanted them to separate. At the time, their six children were between the ages of seventeen and twenty-nine, with the youngest one still living in the family home. Over their years together, Angela reared the children while Mark worked to provide financially for their family. This news was devastating to him because he felt that he'd worked hard all his life and now, when he could slow down, he had no companion and felt he was too old to start again. Because of their financial situation, it wasn't possible for Mark to move out, nor was it possible for him to go away every weekend. He was heartbroken because he was still in love with his wife and felt cast aside, yet he was still stuck in the family home. He was feeling quite hopeless about the future. Although he accepted the fact that their marriage was now over, the agony had become unbearable – he knew that something needed to change, even if his circumstances couldn't.

Unfortunately, continuing to live together further complicates the ending of a relationship.

Whatever the reason for staying together, there is no doubt that when one or both people want to separate, being forced to stay living in the same home for an indeterminable period can seem like a prison sentence with no hope of parole. Others will only stay together for a short time until things have been finalised, knowing that this might only take a couple of weeks or a few months.

Some couples who are separating will find it easier to be civil to each other. Maybe they had a sound friendship but the passion has gone, or the tension and conflict between them is now over and they feel relief at their decision. Perhaps they know that it will be easier for everyone if they cooperate with each other to get through it. Clearly, this is easier if you know that staying together in the same house has a limited time span, although that's not to say you can't remain on friendly terms after that.

Continuing to live together can be difficult, awkward and almost unbearable at times, and it can become worrisome when you start thinking of how you will manage when a family event comes along, such as a communion, a confirmation, your children's milestone birthdays, a wedding, and so on. This becomes even more complicated for people who do not disclose their separation until they are about to physically part. The burden of keeping the secret is yet another pressure as they maintain the facade of being a couple to the outside world when the reality is entirely different.

In these circumstances it is very important to find outlets, no matter how small, by which you can get some relief from what's happening. Some people find relief when they go to their friend's house for an hour or two or even up to the local pub for a drink or by investing more time in their hobbies, spending more time at work, taking a short holiday, etc. Such distractions are not going to change the situation, but they do give you breathing space. Weekends can be particularly tense as both of you may be around each other more and there is a break from the routine of the week. You may find it awkward and stressful co-habiting when you are no longer a couple, especially when there have been no agreements made between you and your partner about how you will share space and utilities in the home.

It is also arguable whether you can emotionally separate from your partner when you are still living together. You may still share tasks, money and child care. Perhaps due to lack of space or because of the children, you may still be in the same bed. It could appear on the surface that not much has changed. You are still living as a couple, yet you no longer behave as such. It is very normal to find the whole experience confusing because your reality, i.e. that you are separated, has no bearing on the way things are from day to day. This tricky stage of the separation journey will require you to adjust to a new set of circumstances. Your ability to get through this in one piece will depend on various factors like your personality and how you adapt to change (are you quick or slow to adjust?), whether you were the one who wanted the separation or not, and how you negotiate the practical problems that come with having to stay in the same home for the present.

When Emotions Get Out of Hand

Finding yourself in a place or a situation where you do not want to be, where there may be tension and resentment and an underlying anxiety about what is to come, can be similar to living in a pressure-cooker environment. Those who are going through separation can experience a melting pot of mixed and often very intense emotions. In some homes where there is such unhappiness and where people feel trapped, the strong feelings that come from loss can spiral out of control and, even if it has never happened before, someone can lash out by thumping, hitting or kicking, accompanied by verbal abuse.

This reaction is not gender specific, but is more typically initiated by the person who is being left behind. Their violence is a reaction to their feelings of hurt and abandonment rather than a desire to control or dominate. Underlying all this perhaps is their plea, 'Who am I without you?' Afterwards, they may be left with the shock of what they have done, possibly leading to further feelings of guilt, remorse, anger, fear, sadness and shame. What this type of behaviour flags up is the very deep pain this person is experiencing and that support is now needed. Please be aware of your behaviour, and if you feel that you or your partner might be teetering on the edge of violence recognise that emotions are very raw at the moment and that you both need to take care of your own personal safety. The end of a relationship is one of those times in life that calls upon us to demonstrate the most mature of responses, yet it can evoke the most primitive and immature of reactions.

It is worth remembering that, regardless of whether or not court orders are made under the domestic violence legislation, physical and/or sexual violence is a crime. The Gardaí have the power to arrest and charge a person who is violent (see <u>www. legalaidboard.ie</u>).

Living Together after Telling Your Partner that It's Over

As described in Chapter 2, it may have taken you quite some time to decide that you no longer want to be in a relationship with your partner. For whatever reason or reasons, you come to the conclusion that this isn't the relationship for you anymore. You may have tried over and over again to give it a chance and so you began to question your future together. The decision to separate from your partner is so huge that people find themselves swinging back and forth for a long period, alternating between the desire to stay and ending the relationship.

One day you might think, 'It's definitely over for me' and the next day you may be wracked with doubt: 'Ah, sure, things aren't all that bad and might be worse if I left.' This ambivalence is usually about fear – fear of losing money, fear of being on your own, fear of losing the children, fear of not meeting anyone else, etc. However, eventually you will make a decision and the torturous process of figuring out a way to tell your partner begins. It goes without saying that, whatever way you say it, it is likely to bring pain.

There's no way to predict how your partner will react and, if you are a caring person, you will be looking for a gentle way to break the news. Indeed, you may still have mixed feelings about whether it is the right decision at all. It would make sense that you act with certainty (or *not* act until you are certain *enough*). If you act with uncertainty, your partner is more likely to be left with a more fragile and intense grief. In general, the pain of ending a relationship becomes more complicated when the loss is potentially revocable (you are giving off signals that you're not entirely sure this is what you want), as opposed to irrevocable (Gurman and Jacobson 2002).

Another way to look at it is to imagine ripping a plaster off – if you do it slowly the pain is drawn out; if you do it quickly and with firmness the pain is sharp but diminishes after a short while. So if your partner thinks there is a chance that you will change your mind, when the reality is that it is really over for you, you will be prolonging the agony for all. Please be as honest as you can about *why* it is over for you, bearing in mind that you may have to make decisions about how much detail to disclose, especially if you think that certain things will really hurt your partner.

Once you have told them, be prepared for the upset that inevitably comes. For them, it can feel like a bomb has been dropped into their laps and they may be shocked at first, before a wave of emotion washes over them. Sometimes it hits them straight away and sometimes it takes a while. Your partner may have had no idea how you were feeling. Although you may feel huge relief at finally ending the relationship, even so, it is also a sad time for you. It is quite natural also for you to feel quite weighed down with guilt.

> Mick (31): 'My feelings had changed towards my ex, with whom I'd been in a relationship for eight years. One night, when we'd had a few drinks after being out with friends, she said she noticed that I was acting quite strangely towards her. At first, I tried to brush it off, but she kept insisting that something was up and I finally admitted that I was no longer in love with her. I'd been feeling like this for a good while but I'd hoped it was just a phase and I'd get over the hump and I'd fall in love with her again. Not knowing what to say, it took her to confront me and it just came out. We stayed up talking all night – we were both upset but I knew by the time the sun came up that it was the right decision for me to end it.'

If you are uncertain about how you feel, you may try to continue to live with your partner, even after you have voiced your doubts about the relationship and felt yourself swaying more in the direction of ending it – it really does feel like it's over for you. Perhaps it is the case that you cannot yet leave the home because of financial reasons. You may also feel like your ex is trying to influence you into staying and wants to have endless conversations with a view to getting back together. Their behaviour may also change (and this will include being nice and doing things for you) which you may see as an attempt to persuade you to change your mind. This can be particularly irritating and might make you want to push them away even further. They may also have endless questions in their attempt to find a definitive answer to what the problem is and to figure out a solution so you can remain as a couple. This is likely to try your patience, especially if your mind is made up that it is over.

Sometimes, the temptation is to let them continue being nice to you (this might have been what was missing from the relationship and why you subsequently fell out of love). Alternatively, you might not want to upset them even further, or want to avoid risking their anger if you reject what they are offering. Trying to be nice to them in order to keep the peace, without being clear about why you are doing this, can set off a chain of misunderstandings. It can give them false hope which will further prolong their grieving. They may believe that everything is alright again, which will cause you to feel angry and/or frustrated and when they realise that you still no longer want a relationship with them, they will once again feel rejection and shame. You may find your partner quite emotional and you may begin to dread spending time in the home when they are also there. In fact, you may find yourself doing other things that keep you out of your home during this time. That's why it's important that you are clear about your decision before you say anything and, even more importantly, that you stick to it.

If it is over and you continue to live together, it is important to put as much space between you and your ex-partner as possible, physically, emotionally and sexually. Try to be patient with them. It can feel like a juggling act but remember that you will have known for a lot longer that the relationship was over – it may have been a shock for your ex-partner and they are still trying to come to terms with it.

The frustration and anger you feel at not being able to move out can leave you feeling quite negative. Some people describe a sense of hopelessness and despair, which are reasonable reactions to an unreasonable set of circumstances. Not only is your ex-partner perhaps not behaving the way that you believe is best, but you may also have become difficult to live with. In an effort to try to keep it all together, you might attempt to withdraw completely from your ex. The danger of this is you can become isolated from your partner and, if you have them, your children. You can feel 'pushed out' by the rest of the family.

It will come as a huge relief when you are finally in the position to physically separate. However, some people are surprised at how upset they are when the time comes to say goodbye, and they wonder whether they made the right decision and have a moment of self-doubt. This level of emotion is quite normal with such a significant ending. It doesn't necessarily mean that you have made a mistake.

Living Together after Your Partner Tells You that It's Over

Finding out that your partner is no longer in love with you and wants to separate may seem like a shock. Even if you hadn't been getting along, the extent of your partner's feelings might be quite different to yours. You may not have seen your problems as insurmountable or even noticed that there were any problems at all. And so, the early days of finding out that your relationship is over usually brings with it a strong sense of confusion once the initial shock has worn off. You might ask yourself, 'What happened? When did their feelings change? What did I do wrong? Can we fix it?'

You may still be harbouring hope that the relationship can be saved, yet your partner seems determined to separate. Continuing to live in the same home as your ex can be purgatory, like being in a no-man's land. You want them to be in love with you again and for things to go back to normal, and yet there is a real fear that they will actually leave you and you will be left on your own. You partner may be uncooperative and uncommunicative and not be willing to provide you with the reassurance that you now need. The more they pull away from you and act like they have already left the home, the more you may be tempted to try to get them to talk to you. This is underpinned by a natural yet deep anxiety when you feel like something you value is being taken away.

Perhaps there is a distance between you now that wasn't there before and your partner may not be interested in what you say anymore. When you can't talk freely about your feelings, it may seem like you're walking on eggshells, tip-toeing around your partner. It's lonely without them. Trying to keep it all together, to make an effort, to be there for them (after all, you don't want to let them go) puts enormous pressure on you. If you have found yourself in this position, you are probably dealing with all kinds of insecurities around not being good enough, and your natural desire is to protest your worth to your partner. At the same time, you may also want to withdraw from them because you are so hurt. You may try many times to 'win over' or reason with your partner about why you should stay together. Believing that the relationship still has merit or worth can be a type of denial.

Janet (39): 'When my husband told me that he was unhappy and was thinking of leaving, I couldn't quite believe it. We had two small children under the age of four and I thought we were happy enough. Okay, we weren't getting enough

111

sleep and had very little 'us' time, but I just thought it was one of those things that every couple went through. When I realised how unhappy he was, I started making more of an effort. He hadn't made himself clear that he was leaving, just said he wasn't happy and he didn't think we should stay together. I took it as a sign that he just wanted to change things in our relationship. Imagine my shock when, two months later, I got a solicitor's letter. That's when it hit me, that he was serious.'

Letting Go

Relationships involve two people and, if the love is over for one, finally the other will arrive at a place where they will run out of steam, when they realise that it is futile to keep up the effort of trying to resurrect what has died. This is a low point, but it can also bring relief to both. Believe it or not, this can be the moment when recovery begins (Webb 1998).

The amount of energy that is expended in trying to keep hope alive would surprise all but those who are going through it. Imagine you had only eight pints of energy every day and think about how much energy you put into trying to rescue a relationship that you desperately want to hold on to – many people who get to this point will admit that it's never really out of their minds, that they find it hard to concentrate on anything else and nearly impossible to keep to normal, daily routines. Everything else pales into insignificance when faced with an ending like this. When a person finally stops investing their energy in saving a relationship, they become more in touch with their own feelings about the loss, and their grieving and healing starts. Reaching this point is greatly helped by not having to live with your ex-partner, but if circumstances mean that you must continue to live together, there are some practical steps you can take to make things easier for both you and your ex-partner, and your children.

How to Live Together When You Are No Longer a Couple

Regardless of whether you have decided to stay together indefinitely or whether it is for a determined period of time, you will still have to negotiate a practical way to live in the same home. Even though you are no longer together and may both be at a point where you're more or less on the same side, it can be stressful sharing the same home as two individuals (with or without children) and increased stress does have a tendency to lower tolerance levels. Any goodwill that exists between the couple will be of significant importance during this time spent in the twilight zone when they are adjusting to change. Their ability to acknowledge each other's need for space and to communicate respectfully will influence how well it can work between them.

Controlling Your Feelings and Behaviour

There is no wrong way or right way to feel, but note that feelings quickly become behaviours that aren't always healthy or beneficial. We tend to have predictable patterns that lie hidden in our subconscious. As children, we learn to cope with certain situations by behaving in a certain way. For example, as a child, if you were frightened by your parent's anger, you might have found yourself becoming angry yourself to ward off the threat, or you may have become placating to that adult in order to calm down their anger and restore peace. In either case, your behaviour had a purpose, i.e. to eliminate the threat. Our young bodies would have also produced hormones to help us when we were on high alert. These 'fight or flight' hormones would have given us the energy to react. When something came at us that we didn't like or trust, or that we believed would hurt us in some way, our reaction was instinctive, at gut level. As adults, though, we have free will and we can make choices about how to regard a possible threat and subsequently respond to it.

The difference between *reacting* and *responding* is that reacting tends to have a strong emotional charge over which you feel you have little or no control (and causes you to behave impulsively), whilst responding is more about pausing to consider what's happening inside you, to name the emotion and what's causing it, giving you a chance to take control of the impulse.

Consider for a moment if you have ever found yourself in a position where you have been annoyed with someone and you became so angry that it scared you? Do you know why you became so angry? Was it instant or did it take a few minutes? Did you feel like you had a choice about that feeling? How strong was the motivation of your anger? Was your reaction useful to the situation?

You may have felt like you didn't have much choice but to behave the way you did at the time. However, if you can stand back from reacting to an impulsive feeling, its intensity or charge usually decreases in less than a minute, thereby allowing you to take some control over your feelings and reducing the chance that you will do or say something you might later regret. That's why counting to ten, and then counting to ten again, before you respond helps.

If you find that your behaviour is alarming you, I would recommend that you get some professional help. The reason I say this is because sorting out the practicalities of a separation requires you to be logical and practical and you cannot do this when you are overwhelmed by emotion.

All through the journey of separation, you will be met with a plethora of emotions and behaviours that you may not ever recall having experienced with such intensity before. Being able to manage your more difficult feelings will help you to keep things on an even keel so that the practicalities of a separation agreement or divorce settlement, or even the dividing of possessions, can be seen to in a balanced manner. In their book *The Healing Journey through Divorce* (1999), Phil Rich and Lita Linzer Schwartz have outlined a series of questions that can help you to get a better understanding of and handle on your emotions:

- What is the hardest part of your current situation?

- In general, how are you handling things?

114

- How are you treating your (ex-)partner? Are your interactions appropriate, or are they making a difficult situation even more difficult?

- How are you treating yourself? Are you taking care of yourself, or are you engaging in activities that you know are not in your own best interests?

- Look hard at your behaviours. Are there things you're doing that you shouldn't be doing?

- Look hard again. Are there things you are saying that you shouldn't be saying?

- What are you doing that's productive – that's *helping* the situation?

- What are you doing that's counterproductive – that's making the situation *worse*?

- Look back at what you've just written. Are you satisfied with the way you're handling things, or are there changes you'd like to make? (p. 29)

Negotiating

Growing up, we learned about rules and boundaries, both from our parents and other authority figures. Those rules are often put there to protect us and keep us from harm. At times like this, when the future is uncertain and routines are cast aside, it is important, more than ever, that there is an agreed system in place that everyone understands and that is adhered to.

As adults, we are expected to be able to negotiate with each other so that each gets something from the outcome. With emotions at an all-time high, it can be difficult to sort things out without a sense of there being a winner or a loser, but it is possible. Trying to come to some agreement about how you are going to live in the same home as your ex-partner requires good communication, that is, really listening to your ex-partner's needs and wishes as well as expressing your own.

If your ex-partner feels heard and acknowledged, they are far more likely to hear what you have to say when your turn comes around.

Prepare beforehand what you want to get out of a discussion with your ex – write it down if it makes it clearer. Become aware of your mood leading up to the negotiation meeting – are you panicky, angry, tired, nervous or anxious? If you are feeling any of these, is it possible for you to calm yourself down so that you have more control over what it is you want to say without becoming too emotional?

Make sure your phones are turned off and there are no other distractions, e.g. children, television, internet. You both need to keep a clear head throughout the discussion(s) and if you feel it is getting heated, stop for an agreed time before resuming. This may take a few minutes or a few days, but make a definite agreement to come back to the discussion, and stick to it.

> Sue (38): 'I knew we had some stuff to sort out, like who was going to be responsible for walking/feeding the dogs and if my husband would agree to take the children on his own every second weekend as if we had, in fact, physically separated. He was away a lot and I rarely had any 'me' time. If I'd asked him to stay with the kids while I went off with my friends, he'd usually think up some excuse, i.e. work or that he'd other arrangements made – I hated that about him! I'd usually end up in tears and he'd be angry then.
>
> I was nervous about this and took a few deep breaths before we started. I asked him what did he want and did my best to listen, although I felt like interrupting a few times because I felt some of what he was asking for was unreasonable. But this wasn't a time for slagging him off or defending my corner. When he finished, it was my turn. He did listen to me until I'd finished and I didn't cry because I knew he wanted stuff from me too so his life could be more bearable.

I commented that we were both looking for a bit of peace. We decided that we'd each give each other two things from the lists that we'd both made, and that we'd stick to it and that we'd sit down again two weeks later and see how we were doing.'

Sue and her ex-husband both recognised that pulling against each other wasn't going to get them anywhere and they were both concerned about how the fighting would affect their children. A friend of Sue's had recommended that, when she was trying to reach agreement with her husband, she pretend there was someone else in the room who she really respected and this would help her to stay calm and to speak with dignity.

Practical Decisions

What kind of agreements do people make when they're continuing to live together for the immediate or long-term future? Every household has its own arrangements and each individual has their own role (or several roles), whether they are the person who earns the money, puts out the bins or does the shopping. I would suggest that you now think of your partner as a housemate with whom you are sharing space. Start with the following basics:

Sleep Separately

Do you have a spare bedroom or other space that can be converted to accommodate this? People come up with all kinds of excuses to avoid separate beds – they don't want to put the children out or there isn't enough room in the house/apartment, but this is one of the key ways to detach yourself from your ex when one or both of you cannot move out of the home for the time being. Couples still have sex when they are breaking up. Ironically, the intensity of the emotions around breaking up can often be the catalyst that brings them together sexually. Even if you aren't getting on, there may still be moments when the desire to have sex is strong and it can be a source of comfort. Please avoid this if at all possible, because it just adds to the confusion for both of you.

Chores

Every home has a list of tasks that need to be done in order to keep it in working order. Dinner still has to be made, clothes have to be washed and ironed, children have to be put to bed and the bins have to be put out. How do you both feel is the best way to manage this? Do you eat separately, do your own washing and ironing and alternate the days when you have time with the children? Do your previously shared possessions, even down to the tins in the cupboard, get split down the middle? Sometimes it is easier if things stay the same for practical reasons. However, as mentioned, try to approach things as if your ex is a housemate. It will help you to become more detached over a period of time.

Finances

In some couples, only one partner works or one person may be earning a greater income than the other. The couple may have a shared bank account from which both withdraw money. If that is the case, separation is the time for opening up separate accounts. At some point, you will have to agree on finances with your ex-partner. If it is possible to do this before you physically separate, it will make the long-term official separation or divorce procedure more straightforward.

Children

A word of caution – do not try to sort out your differences in front of your children. They will be affected by what's going on between you. You are still their parents, even if you are no longer a couple. It is quite common for children to be used as messengers in the family home: 'Tell your mum ...'; 'Tell your dad...'. By doing this, you are forcing them into a cauldron of upset that they don't deserve. Yes, it may be easier to ask them to do the message carrying, but if you have something to say to your ex-partner and you can't speak it, leave a note or send a text or email.

Health

This may sound obvious but it is really important that you take care of your health during this period. The pain of a relationship ending is very stressful and the temptation may be to drink too much, comfort eat or take drugs. Exercise stimulates the production of endorphins, which lift your mood as well as being good for your body and helping you to relax and sleep. Healthy food helps to keep you physically healthy and will keep your energy levels up. Sleep can be a problem since your mind can be unable to rest – eating properly and exercising can help to keep sleep problems to a minimum. When you have a lot on your mind, it can help to write it all down and make a promise to yourself that you'll get back to it tomorrow. If you find that you have a persistently low mood (two weeks or more) or ongoing panic attacks, it is recommended that you see your doctor.

Separate Schedules

It's not always practical but some people say that it helps when you're not spending so much time together in the house. For example, is it possible for one person to be up and gone before the other gets up in the morning? Can you organise to see friends or play sport at times when your ex-partner is at home? Is it possible to arrange to do separate things in the evening or at the weekend, meaning that only one of you is at home? If you are entertaining in the family home, think about how good your relationship is with your ex-partner. Can it withstand social exposure? Will your friends feel comfortable with you both? Or is it better to see your friends away from the home altogether?

This is, of course, not ideal, but it can be the most convenient arrangement if there is a sizeable amount of tension still there between you.

New Relationships

Some people move on from their relationship quite quickly and meet someone new, feeling that they're ready to start again. They see a new relationship as a second chance. However, their ex-partner and especially children are likely to see it quite differently. This is one area that can cause huge upset, especially when introducing your new partner to children.

It goes without saying that it is not a good idea to introduce a new partner to your ex or your children, especially in the initial stages. If you are still living with your ex, please be respectful and conduct the new relationship away from the family home. In addition, phone calls, texting and emailing to and from your new partner can be very distressful for others. You may feel it is your right, now that you are no longer a couple, but it's easier for everyone if you keep it discreet.

Your Whereabouts

Even though you may now be more or less on the same page regarding your agreement to separate, couples do not tend to detach that easily or quickly. Part of the challenge that faces a couple, even after they have physically separated, is to actually live their lives separately without wanting to know the nuances of what is going on in their ex-partner's life. If you still have some feelings towards your partner, it is natural to wonder about their whereabouts; when you are still living together, their comings and goings are more obvious.

On the one hand, you may feel your ex-partner has no right to know what you are getting up to now you have separated. Yet, if you are sharing a home and have children together, you do have an obligation to notify them, broadly speaking anyway, of your whereabouts. This doesn't mean that you have to give them a blow-by-blow account of what you are getting up to in your life (although some people like to tell their ex how well they are doing now they are not together anymore. This is bred perhaps from insecurity more than anything else. If you are doing this, please consider how helpful this is to maintaining harmony in the home). On the other hand, if you do not give your ex any information whatsoever, and/or there was little trust in your relationship with them anyway, they will be left speculating. If you find yourself pre-occupied with your ex-partner's whereabouts, please do whatever you can to distract yourself. This repetitive, almost obsessive, thinking will wear you out emotionally and physically. All it will do is heighten your own insecurities and anxiety about the separation.

Learning to stand back from being part of each other's lives, including discussing your day-to-day experiences, has to be one of the most difficult things for a couple to navigate when they have to share the same house, because they are witness to the separate life of the other in their comings and goings. They need to respect their new relationship with each other and each other's need for just the right amount of space and just the right amount of information, which will have a different context to when they were a couple.

Attitude

It may seem like an uphill battle at times, but do your best to maintain a positive attitude. The ending of a relationship can be awkward and tense but the situation need not remain so difficult. If you work together and keep your children's welfare as your primary focus, things will improve. If you do not have children, there may be less motivation to keep your shared space emotionally hassle-free. Perhaps you really need to irritate each other so much that by the time you move apart it's a huge relief. However, knowing that you are doing your best does convey a certain dignity and regard for yourself and what you once had with your ex.

Chapter 7

Friends and Family of Separating Couples

When someone gets sick, care and attention is focused on them. Anyone who has ever had a family member in hospital will know how exhausting it can become, from the visits to and fro every day to responding to concerned friends and relatives looking for updates on the patient's welfare. It can all become quite draining after a while as much of your energy becomes devoted to the care of the patient.

We can draw similarities between caring for a sick relative or friend and looking after someone close to us who is experiencing the end of a serious relationship. You want to do everything you can to help them and, especially in the initial stages, you may get drawn into protecting and caring for the separating person(s), possibly finding yourself becoming quite emotional at times too. This chapter is an important one to include in this book because, as someone who is close to the separated person, you will also be affected. As a caring human being you are likely to be sensitive to the emotions of others and it's quite likely that some of their pain will be taken on by you as well.

What is important is how you can support your friend or family member with compassion and understanding, while taking care of yourself in the process, without becoming overwhelmed.

Of course, the separating couple are right there at the coalface. But you are also likely to experience many of the feelings that accompany grief, as well as trying to support one or both of the separating parties and any children involved. One way to describe it is that a separation is like a fire burning in the grate. It doesn't just warm up the fireplace but affects the general temperature in the room. Naturally, the more the relationship meant to you, as a family member or friend, the closer you will be standing to the grate and the greater the intensity of feelings you will experience at this time.

As a friend or family member of a couple who are separating, it can be awkward for you, especially in the initial stages. If you have had a good relationship with the separating couple up until now, it can also be difficult to figure out how to continue a relationship with both people without one or both of them feeling betrayed. You may also be at a loss to understand how the relationship came to an end if it seemed a good one to you. Or you might wonder how your friend's partner could have left him/her, someone you're so fond of.

It's also hard to remain impervious to gossip when we start hearing tales about what 'really' went on in the relationship. Do your best to remain outside of it. People's opinions are subjective at best and news gets distorted when it is passed from one person to another.

In an ideal world, the separating couple would be able to acknowledge everyone's awkwardness and be okay about their own friends and family staying in touch with their ex, if that is what they wish to do. This does happen sometimes and, when it does, it reduces the pressure and stress for family and friends. However, the ending of a significant relationship is so painful that it is hard for a couple to consider others when they are so overwhelmed themselves.

Some people find themselves feeling uncomfortable when they find out that a relationship of someone they know has broken up – if their own relationship isn't very happy, they may start questioning whether they want to continue in a relationship with their current partner. People can feel that by associating with the separating couple they'll somehow catch the 'separating bug'. Consequently, they start putting distance between themselves and the separating couple and friendships begin to disintegrate. You may also have a relationship with the separated couple based on the fact that they were a couple and you did 'couple' things together. You may have very little in common with them otherwise.

Right Vs Wrong – The Moral Dilemma

Even though we are less influenced nowadays by the Church, and separation and divorce have become more of a cultural norm, people will still have strong opinions about marriage and whether it is right to separate if a relationship is no longer working. If you have strong beliefs that a couple should stay together, even if they are unhappy, will it really be possible for you to suspend your own code of beliefs and principles to support a friend or family member if they decided to separate? Although separation has been possible in this country for a long time, many couples stayed together even if their marriage was miserable. Many will continue to remain in marriages that are no longer working, but separation and divorce are becoming more accepted as options for dealing with a relationship that is over. Separation could be seen as the easy way out, but in my experience of working with people who have found themselves in this position, it is a very tough journey and people do not make this decision lightly. They agonise over how it will affect their families and the shame and guilt they feel at the thought of putting them through this. They worry about what their friends will think of them and if they will remain friends at all as a result. This adds to the burden of their sense of failure that the relationship didn't work out.

If you come from a close family or a close circle of friends, it is more likely that the separating couple are an integral part of your lives, in terms of socialising and supporting each other. Therefore, it can be awkward at the very least as the group adjusts to the loss of the couple, even if individuals within the group remain friends with both people involved.

Giving Advice

Certainly not in all cases, but in many, the separated person(s) will want to talk and ask for your advice. It feels natural, as part of you helping them, to give them advice on what you think is the best course of action. Please bear in mind that, however well-meaning your intentions, this is not necessarily the most helpful thing to do. People have a habit of making up their own minds no matter how confused they are and you may feel frustrated if they seem to consistently go against your advice. Alternatively, they may take your advice if it is what they would have done themselves and blame you later if it was the wrong thing to do. Sometimes you are a confidante to both and may know certain information that is not available to the person who is looking for your help. This places you in a very difficult position because if you disclose what you know, you may feel like you are betraying a confidence – yet you do want to help. Try to consider where your limits are in terms of what you are comfortable knowing. That way, you will avoid the awkwardness of keeping a secret or having to be the bearer of someone else's news.

If you are approached for advice, take a deep breath. Remember you are their support and, unless you are an expert in the area in which your advice is being sought, try to present options and food for thought instead of telling them what to do. It is perfectly okay to say you don't know what they should do but that you are a willing ear if they want to talk it through. They may be very upset and distressed and seem very confused, and of course you will want to help them. But rather than rush to a solution, pause and acknowledge their feelings, because when feelings are identified they lessen in their intensity and people often say they calm down and things become clearer. For example:

Separating Person (SP): I don't know what to do. He said that he'd take the children on Tuesday but now he's saying he can't. Is this what it's going to be like? What do you think I should do?

Friend/family member (F/F): It must be very confusing at the moment and now you're also feeling let down. And you're wondering if you can depend on him again.

SP: Yeah, my head is wrecked from all this and now I can't rely on him to do what he said he'd do. So what do I do?

F/F: It seems to me like you think you should be doing something, so what are your options?

By giving the question back to the separating person, you are allowing them to take responsibility for any action they decide to take, even if it is different to what you would do yourself. Help them to walk around their options by asking open-ended questions. These are questions that start with who, what, where, how or when. Sometimes when we ask 'Why?' it can come across as critical rather than curious, so avoid this one if you can. Using open questioning can help the person to explore their possibilities with a view to making a decision.

Adult Children of Separating Parents

Adult children of a separating couple can believe that because they are now grown up and no longer dependent on their parents they should be okay about their parents separating. However, parental separation can be very upsetting for them too, as upsetting as it would be for younger children.

If your parents are separating, although you may understand why they are doing it (and you might even feel relieved if there had been ongoing tension between your mum and dad), you will still feel a huge loss that they are now going their separate ways. They may never have been openly in conflict and the news may come as a shock. Even if they hadn't been affectionate with each other for some time, it would be quite natural to think that because they've stayed together for so long they would continue to do so. It may even be embarrassing for you that they are separating. Just remember that your parents may feel like they are letting you down, yet they think that it is untenable for them to stay together.

And what will it mean for you as their child? In an ideal world, they would sort out their problems without involving you, but parents can lean on their adolescent and adult children, often treating them as confidantes, and you might find yourself in the awkward situation of feeling quite torn or uncertain about what you hear – after all, it can be uncomfortably painful to hear negative things being said about the other parent. Sometimes we are closer to one parent than to the other. Regardless of why this is, some adult children, like their younger counterparts, can feel like they are under pressure to take sides. They can feel that they are turning into chameleons, being one person with their dad and another person with their mum.

The family operates as a system, with each individual playing their part. For example, perhaps one child plays the part of the responsible one and makes sure everyone is okay, and another child is the clown who always makes the family laugh, and yet another is the sensitive one in the family who always seemed to be the one who was most upset or troubled when something happened. It is during vulnerable times, like separation and divorce, that these roles can become heightened or intensified. Children (even as adults) often won't complain because they feel they will only be adding to the upset and so they either become withdrawn or become the caregivers in the family, taking care of everyone else and soothing their distress, while ignoring their own personal pain. Take a moment to consider your role in your family. If your parents are going through a separation, how is it affecting you?

You might find that one parent is relieved whilst the other is completely devastated. As their child, you may feel under pressure to 'sort it out' and at the same time want to pull away from the stress of it all. This is your parents' relationship – their issues should be kept between them and you have the right to love them both.

In theory, family relationships do not end with separation or divorce; they are just renegotiated. However, in some cases, the distress of the separation and the subsequent taking of sides can mean that one parent becomes isolated from the rest of the family or there may be a split down the middle and the family moves into different camps. It is a shame when this happens, but it would seem that the family are grieving as a unit, and the feelings of grief within the family, which include anger and confusion, will mirror what is happening to the parents' relationship.

You may also wonder about how family occasions like Christmas will be managed from now on. Will it be very awkward? There are lots of important things to consider when something like this happens and confusion and panic in the family, especially in the initial stages, is quite normal. Planning is very important when it comes to family occasions so that no one feels left out, so, perhaps in September, a decision could be made about arrangements for Christmas. I know it seems like a lot of notice but tension builds up when decisions are left until the last minute and one or more people in the family can be left hurt, disappointed and left out. Knowing in good time beforehand gives people a chance to make other plans if they are not going to be spending time together on Christmas Day.

> Lizzie (40): Ever since I can remember, my parents' relationship had been difficult. My mother and myself were close growing up as Dad was away a lot with work. There was talk a long time ago about them separating but it took about eight years for it to actually happen. When they finally separated,

129

everyone seemed to be handling it well. Myself and my brother and sister managed Christmas and other events by making sure that there were always one or two of us with each parent so no one would feel left out. This arrangement worked fine until my brother got engaged. His wedding was taking place near my house and both my parents wanted to come and stay with me. But my house only has two bedrooms and they hadn't seen each other since the day they separated. Over the months, as the wedding preparations were getting underway, I began to look forward to it less and less, dreading how I would tell one of them, 'Sorry but the other one has already asked me to stay ...' I knew the one who didn't get picked would be hurt and it would upset their day but I was tying myself up in knots and eventually burst into tears with the tension. My old friend was with me when it happened and she knew what it was like growing up in my family. She said, 'Your mum and dad have separated, but have you?' I realised in that moment that I was still behaving the same way as I did when I was younger – worrying about how to handle them and make it okay for everyone. Eventually when I calmed down, I told my parents that they were both welcome to stay and let them decide themselves. Even though they didn't do so well as a couple, they were both loving parents to us all. Mum came two days before the wedding and Dad made other arrangements. But he asked could he come the day after the wedding and Mum went to stay with a friend nearby. They behaved cordially to each other on the day. We were so proud!'

When Your Child Separates

Parents of a separating couple can deeply mourn the loss of the relationship if they have been close to their child's ex-partner. They may have seen the problems in their child's relationship and tried to warn them, to no avail. Many fear that if civility isn't maintained it will mean that they will be cut off from their grandchildren. To date, sadly, grandparents do not have any legal rights to their grandchildren. Unfortunately, grandparents of the parent who only has part-time custody or access to children will suffer in particular, which is a huge loss to them and to the children.

How parents of separating couples behave in the initial stages of a break-up can influence their own child's, as well as their grandchildren's, healing. This is often down to being able to keep a civil (if not friendly) relationship with your child's ex-partner. Grandparents can be an incredible support to their children as well as helping to provide security and stability for their grandchildren. They cannot replace parents but they can give grandchildren a sense of belonging to a wider extended family.

Some of the common mistakes grandparents can make are bad-mouthing, criticising and blaming the ex-son-in-law or -daughter-in-law, jumping to conclusions about what caused the relationship to end, or immediately trying to seize control of the crisis and ending up making their own child too dependent on them in the long run. Your child may be the one who misbehaved or had been abusive in their relationship, thus leading to its demise. You may have a close relationship with your son- or daughter-in-law and feel awful for what your child has done. If you are in their confidence, you may find out things about your child that cause you hurt and anguish. However, your child may expect your loyalty and you can be there for them, which is quite different to saying, 'I agree with what you did.'

You might actually end up blaming yourself for what's happening and agonising over whether you could have done anything to prevent the split. As a parent, you will worry about your child's future and, naturally, you will take on some of their pain as if it were your own. Parents do have a tendency to question how they might have contributed to their children's difficulties, perhaps by their own parenting or mistakes they made in their own marriages which may have affected their children. Blame doesn't really matter or help. It just gets in the way. The answer is that there is no such thing as the perfect relationship and you are not to blame. Please keep some perspective – things happen in relationships that threaten them and some don't survive.

Thirty or forty years ago if their marriage was in trouble people just knuckled down and got on with it. In today's world people don't have to stay in an unhappy relationship. Perhaps you might think that some relationships finish too easily, with little effort or time invested in repairing them. Perhaps your own relationship went through rocky patches and you got through it eventually. It can be hard for parents to stand by their children and not judge their decisions, especially when they disagree with what is happening. You can support your child and give them your strength without compromising your own values.

On the other hand, you may not have liked your child's choice of partner and be secretly relieved and even pleased that it's now over and you no longer have to tolerate them. It is important at this time that you do not use this as an opportunity to air your dislike of them. Even though the relationship is now over, your child may still be yearning for them either consciously or unconsciously and to criticise their ex may only intensify already painful feelings. The best thing you can do for them is *not* take sides. I know this can be difficult but, long term, it will help your child to move on and I'm sure that is at the heart of what you would want for them.

When Your Sibling Separates

As with your parents, you may or may not have liked your brother or sister's choice of partner. If you liked them, you will feel sad that they are no longer part of your family, even though you might still consider yourselves as friends. Friends share confidences and if you are privy to information that might affect your sibling, you may have mixed feelings about how to handle it without feeling like you're betraying your brother or sister.

If your sibling was the one to end the relationship, you may feel the subtle pull from their ex to 'talk sense into them'. On the other hand, you might find yourself quite puzzled and perhaps angry if their ex was the one to finish it. Either way, you are likely to experience difficult feelings because you are also emotionally involved. Recognise your own feelings and then put them aside as this is a time when your sibling will need your support, even if you aren't very close.

If you didn't have a close relationship with your sibling's ex, it can be much more straightforward as you will only feel the need to support your sibling. However, if there are children involved aunts and uncles (similar to grandparents) do worry about losing contact with their nephews and nieces and how they are going to keep a civil and respectful enough relationship with the other parent so that they can keep in contact with the children. What can really help here is to avoid finger pointing or apportioning blame to any party, to acknowledge that it is a difficult time for everybody and to keep the focus on the well-being of the children. Even if you don't agree with how one or the other is parenting, you do need to be mindful of the fact that the children's parents may be acting out their own grief through their children. Is it possible to offer your babysitting services to give them a break or to become a trusted confidante for the children who may be struggling to communicate their own hurt?

When Your Friend Separates

As a friend of someone whose relationship is over, there are some very practical things you can do to help and support them through what can be one of the most painful experiences of their lives. It's often difficult to know what to say or do that will be most appropriate. The best thing you can do for them is listen, listen, listen, and encourage them to do small things that make them feel good. Do not promise them anything you cannot deliver and if you have to say no to something, be very clear and as gentle as you can about it.

As mentioned earlier, avoid going down the advice-giving route unless you are an expert in the area. It is quite normal for them to be confused and to reach out to you, asking you what you think, in the hope that they will get some clarity about whatever it is that is bothering them. A simple way to hand it back to them is to say, 'If I was in your position, what would you recommend I should do?'

Of course, criticising or bad-mouthing their ex-partner is discouraged. You may actually feel like doing it or want to say something negative about their ex to show your support and loyalty, but bad-mouthing only adds to negative feelings and serves no useful purpose.

Don't try to push them into doing things, unless they're spending far too much time alone. They may agree to meet you somewhere and then change their minds or forget to show up. It can be upsetting for you when that happens but people going through something as painful as the end of a relationship need time to themselves to sort things out. Their feelings are all over the place and they never know how they're going to feel from one moment to the next. Try to be mindful of this and don't be offended if they don't want to spend time with you at present. If you're in a relationship, being in the company of a happy couple will only remind them of their loss. If you're single, they may find the single life somewhat frightening. Give them space and mention that you'll be there for them when they want to get in touch. They'll usually come back when they're ready to face the world again. Just listen and watch for the clues and be considerate of their needs. This does not exclude you from getting in touch with them to invite them out or dropping them the odd text or email, but also say that you understand if they're not ready, you just thought they might like the idea – no pressure!

How You Can Support Someone Going through a Separation

It is quite natural not to know what to say to someone going through the end of a relationship. Their grief may be so strong that it can feel quite overwhelming to you. At times, you can alternate between feeling frustrated (you love them and want them to feel better and yet they don't seem to be moving on) and wanting to avoid them because spending time with someone who is in such pain over a prolonged period can become quite draining. They may be behaving in one of the following ways, which can be perplexing to you:

- They may be clinging to or yearning for their ex-partner (or clinging onto their children as a substitute for their ex) when they should be letting go. What they need most from you is support, encouragement and permission to move on.

- They may appear to you as having a consistently strong facade ('I'm fine'), yet be very negative. They may make one-sided or unilateral decisions (which perhaps represent an unconscious desire by them to stay in control). For them, to admit to the pain would mean risking vulnerability and falling apart so they deny and protect themselves from publicly admitting to grieving feelings. Deep down they are frightened and are protecting themselves from hurt. Please be aware, whether you are a friend or part of their family, that people mourn loss differently. Not everyone can openly grieve. A person who behaves like this needs to feel validated in their effort to stay strong and independent, and to develop an awareness that real power and control comes from knowing when and how to say 'yes' as well as 'no.'

- Another type of behaviour that can be most puzzling is when the separating person alternates between rejecting their ex-partner and yearning for them. What you can do to help them is to validate their ambivalence (mixed feelings). The separated person is very vulnerable – they may be quite fearful even if they are not showing it. They may find it difficult to let go and so they hold on, even if it is in a negative or destructive fashion. This is also why they engage in 'revenge tactics' or behave in a way that doesn't correspond with what they are saying, for example, a person might say about their ex-partner, 'I don't know what I ever saw in them and am glad to see the back of them', and yet they seem to stay in touch with them anyway.

(Adapted from the keynote address by Janet R. Johnston at the All-Ireland Conference 'An Eye to the Future: Accepting the Changes to Family Life in the New Millenium', 1999.)

When children get caught up in any of these parental behaviours, they will be adversely affected. So it is important, in your role as a support to one or both members of the couple, to avoid adding fuel to the fire by intensifying any of these behaviours. Helping a person to regain (or maintain) their pride and a strong sense of themselves, along with accepting where they are (this means concentrating on their feelings at a given time and not trying to rush them on), will go a long way in helping them to accept this huge change in their lives and, ultimately, to move on. Those who are grieving often feel misunderstood by others and feel under pressure to get over it when they're not quite ready.

Giving Too Much

As someone who is close to a separating person or couple, you will initially want to do whatever you can to help. But a word of caution at this point! Please consider exactly how much help you can offer and do not offer more than you can give – although you want to support, protect and help your family member or friend get over what's happened, anyone going through a grieving process needs you to be consistent. When a person is going through a life change, they look for stability and consistency to help them adjust. You may have quite a lot going on in your own life and have other commitments that take up your time, money and energy. Yet you do not want to appear like you are abandoning them in their hour of need. When you are promising something to someone else, which will bring much greater pressure for you, sooner or later you may become resentful towards them and because their own emotional sensitivity is heightened, they are likely to pick this up. Neither you nor they will feel good about this.

However, part of the adjustment for the separated person is learning to cope on their own and become independent. You cannot be available 24/7 anyway, because you have your own life. Perhaps you could say, 'I'm sorry I'm not free at the moment to give you the time you need, can we agree a time that will suit us both later?'

If they need a place to stay or money to tide them over, think first about what you can freely give without any huge loss to yourself. A well-thought-out offer may go something like this: 'If you need a place, I can put you up for 2–3 days or a weekend' or 'I can lend you €x amount but I will need it back – when will you be able to return it to me?' Both offers are specific in terms of the time frame. Just remember that this is a transitional time for them and they may not necessarily pay too much heed to what was agreed. It's not that they don't respect what you're saying, but their life is one big blur at the moment.

If your friend or family member needs to stay with you longer or is not making any move to leave, it is up to you to address this with them, being respectful of both positions (yours and theirs). You might say, 'I know you're in a bad place at the moment but I need my space back and I was wondering what's happening.'

If they haven't returned the loan of money (and this can be awkward in any type of friendship, regardless of the circumstances) you might have to say, 'I lent you money and we agreed it would be returned by now. I need it myself at the moment and I'm curious about when I am getting it back.'

Can you see why it's important not to agree to give more (whether it's time, money or your home) than you can? Relationships can be lost when boundaries are overstepped and knowing your own limits will protect a friendship in the long run, although it may feel difficult to do so at the time. Doing too much can be as detrimental as doing too little as it has a tendency to breed over-dependency. One of the main things you can do for a separated person is to encourage renewed independence and self-confidence.

Chapter 8

Formalising Separation

One of the key stages of separation is when the couple finally decide to physically part. As mentioned in Chapter 6, it is arguably impossible to emotionally detach from each other when you are still sharing the same home. But the physical separation of a couple, even though it is a more task-focused part of the journey when we are required to keep our heads on our shoulders, is also inclined to trigger intense feelings of loss. If you have moved beyond the initial shock and now realise that your relationship is truly over, formally dividing your lives becomes a necessary task, whether this is worked out between you or you formalise the agreement using professionals.

Each person will have to contend with the emotions relating to letting go of their partner; as pointed out, this can be painful even for the person who decided to leave. Dividing up joint belongings, assets and liabilities will have a financial consequence, but may also have an emotional impact if things have sentimental value. Even if you agree who gets what in a mostly amicable manner, making decisions about how things get divided does tend to sharpen the sense of loss and pain. When there are children involved, the couple must also face reaching an agreement as to how to share parenting and childcare arrangements.

There are several options available now to achieve a formal separation – if a couple can agree between them as much as possible, there may be little need for outside help, i.e. mediation, collaborative law, solicitors/barristers, and so on. The route that a couple take largely depends on how well they are communicating with each other when they get to this stage. Separation, whether it is out of the blue or has been coming for a while, will naturally bring up fears for the future. Regardless of who made the decision to finish the relationship, the couple will now find themselves in unknown territory, and their actions have unknown results and unknown consequences. Will there be enough and what are our entitlements? How will I/we survive? Will we have to sell the family home? How will we sort out custody and access arrangements for the children? Will the division of assets be fair and equitable to all? And will we be able to agree on what is fair anyway?

Timing Is Key

It is difficult to know when to start sorting out practical matters during such a painful and confusing time. Sometimes the decision about when to start is taken out of your hands when your partner initiates proceedings and there may be little choice left but to respond. In an ideal world, we would wait until the worst of the feelings have passed and we have a clearer head – after all, there are important decisions to be made. But the reality is that someone is going to want this sooner or later, and that's when they get the ball rolling. The hard work that usually accompanies physically separating may be a focus in itself to get through an emotional period and satisfy the need to 'do something', but making decisions when you are *extremely* emotional is inadvisable – these decisions are often regretted later because they were impulsive and were made in reaction to emotion, rather than being logically thought through.

John (40): 'Things were bad between us for three years since the birth of our son. It got to a stage where I was sleeping in the spare room and we were rowing all the time, usually about the kids, and we had no sex. I also lost my job during it all and, although I found another one, we still weren't happy. After one big argument about a month before Christmas my ex told me that it was over for her. I was shocked, but in a strange way I agreed with her. There was nothing left between us anymore except that we had children together. Still, I was sad and worried because I didn't know how we were going to afford to live in two separate houses. I tried not to think about it. I think I was in denial for a bit – I couldn't picture myself living without my family. My wife and I had been together since we were sixteen. It just didn't seem real. This all happened at the end of November and, because of the kids and Christmas, it was agreed that I would move out in late January so they wouldn't remember Christmas as a bad time.

A few weeks later, I arrived home after my Christmas party and had a few drinks on board. She was sitting on the couch looking happy with herself and something snapped in me. I was miserable and she was happy. It just wasn't right. She'd dumped me and got to keep the house, the kids and a few bob in the bank. I didn't think I was capable of rage but it was probably fuelled and distorted by drink. I remember thinking, 'I don't even want to separate – it was her choice.' We ended up having another massive row and I ran upstairs and packed a bag and stayed with my mother. I couldn't go back after that. Christmas was ruined for everyone and I still feel guilty about putting us all through that, even though it was five years ago.

The ironic thing was that, at my son's communion this year, she admitted to me that on the night I left she had been pleased that we were keeping the kids as our focus in spite of our differences and was proud of the way we were putting them first. That's why she looked happy. I felt like such a fool!'

Unfortunately, some couples become locked into attacking, accusing or blaming each other. It becomes difficult to be fair and objective when you are feeling defensive or angry and hurt. Instead, the argument is drawn out, making it impossible to negotiate or agree on anything. Separation isn't fair – everyone is losing something, and your sense of loss can *seem* more acute for you than it is for your partner. But don't be under any illusion that they are not deeply affected either.

Lara (39): 'I found out my husband was having an affair and he wanted to end our relationship in order to be with her. I felt terribly hurt and betrayed by him but knew that, even if he had wanted to stay in our relationship and work at it, I would find it impossible to forgive and forget. Still, I was devastated .... I hadn't married him and moved halfway around the world just to be abandoned like that. I was dreadfully homesick and because of his job we were going to be abroad for another few years anyway. Maybe my unhappiness made him unhappy; who knows? There were so many unanswered questions and things we didn't talk about that would have helped me understand what led to him having an affair. I just needed to get home as quickly as possible, but at the time I remember thinking, 'He's got everything – the girl, a home, his job.' Nothing would change for him. Instead, I lost everything – my husband, my home, my job (because I was moving back), my life!

We divorced four years later and, because of the geographical distance, we didn't meet again until the divorce was being finalised. Both of us had moved on with our lives and were in new relationships. We agreed to meet for lunch 'for closure'. He apologised for what had happened, admitting he still loved me at the time and didn't want me to leave, even though he had done this terrible thing. He explained that, for him, he didn't think that our relationship could be salvaged after what had happened and was at a loss to know how to fix it. I remember feeling very angry when he said it. If he loved me, how could he have gone off with another woman? It just didn't make sense. But I was smart enough to realise I was getting the apology I deserved and, even though all that time had passed, I needed to hear it. Because my anger and hurt wasn't so intense anymore, I didn't feel as defensive or have any strong desire to attack him verbally. I let him finish and we both fell silent. It was an important moment in my life. I could even say, 'Thanks for apologising; that was a nice thing to do' and I smiled at him.

I don't know whether that encouraged him to keep talking but he then went on to say how his own life took a turn after I left. He had previously been very ambitious and was doing well at work but our separation affected him more than he thought it might, or than I even knew. For two years, he had lost his confidence and doubted himself; poor professional decisions on his part meant that he was moved sideways rather than promoted. Honestly, I was sorry to hear that. Maybe somewhere along the line I forgave him without realising it. I'm not a spiritual person, but I think that conversation was healing for me.'

Feelings are a prominent force on the separation journey. They influence our thoughts and behaviours, sometimes adversely. We leave the relationship perhaps believing we are the victims of a crime that has been committed, that there has been some injustice done and that we are doing penance for a something we didn't deserve. That may be so. But to believe that you are the only loser, that your ex comes out on top, has little to do with reality. There are no winners.

One way to prepare yourself for negotiating a formal separation agreement is to consider things from another angle. Think less about what has happened (for instance, your partner having an affair) and more about how you are feeling about it. So, for example, rather than blaming your partner for the affair and trying to hurt them as you have been hurt, another way to deal with it is to explain to your partner how their actions have affected you – 'I'm hurt and heartbroken.' Attacking, blaming and criticising leaves little room for progress.

Refusing to start looking at the options open to you when it really is time to start negotiating how you are going to move forward is a mistake. Yes, you might be sad and afraid because of what's happened and what's ahead, but burying your head in the sand and hoping it will all go away will only prolong what you are already going through (and give you more pain).

Planning

Naturally, the more a couple can agree on together and by themselves, the easier reaching a formal agreement will be. Most people will want to separate in a cost-efficient way that will not drain away all their finances.

Unfortunately, this may not be possible if your partner is unwilling, hostile or just unavailable. However, you can do the following exercise on your own. It will have the added benefit of helping you to clear your head and become more focused. Sit down with a pen and paper and work out the following.

- What do I/we need to do in order to separate? (Short-term, medium-term and long-term goals)

- What are the immediate priorities? (Where to live, children, money, pets, etc.)

- What things do I/we want to keep? (Some things may have clearly been yours or your partner's. If there are things that you both liked, make a list of these so that you can negotiate.)

- Who do I/we need to talk to? (This could be anyone from your boss, MABS (the Money, Advice and Budgeting Service), a counsellor, FLAC (Free Legal Advice Centres), a mediator, a solicitor to parents, friends, etc. Make a list of questions you would like to discuss with them.

- How much money do I/we need to live on? (Be realistic here – there may be only a certain amount on the table and you will need to prioritise.)

- If you have to continue to stay in the same home until everything is sorted, what do you need to negotiate with each other in terms of routines, space and behaviour?

Be sure to give yourself the opportunity to reflect on your options and ensure that you avoid making rash decisions. Even though it may have been a while since the decision was made to separate, the practicalities of splitting up can be painful, so take your time.

If you come to agree on the terms of settlement when you separate and, for whatever reason, have these terms made an Order of Court, there is a provision for review of the Order if you go on to divorce. However, in reality, very little is likely to change unless your circumstances have dramatically altered. This is why it is important to ensure that you attend to, and understand, the consequences of everything you are agreeing to (even if you are making an interim agreement).

It may take some time before both of you get to this stage – it is likely that if there is too much conflict there may be no other option but to engage professional help, i.e. mediators, solicitors, etc., from an early stage. A good reference for establishing the most suitable option for your particular circumstances would be to check out the Citizens Information Centre website at www.citizensinformation.ie.

Taking Responsibility

When a decision to separate has been made, distrust is likely to visit the family. In times of uncertainty, people will want to hold on to what they have when they are unsure of what will be taken from them. It can be tempting to start hiding assets and to become evasive in communication. If one person was the sole or chief breadwinner, the other may start wondering if that person is squirreling funds away. Sadly, this does happen in some relationships as people no longer view themselves as a couple, but as two individuals with little or no perceived responsibility for the other. This is why it is important to lay out where you are financially. If you had all your bills and accounts in both names, you should have easy access to your financial affairs. It is *just as likely* that there is nothing sinister going on and any suspicion that this is not the case can have more to do with your own fear of not having enough when you are on your own. Please remember that when the fear is reduced, the fight is reduced.

When we enter unknown territory, it is quite natural for us to feel a sense of panic initially, until we start gathering information that puts us more comfortably in the driver's seat. Consider for a moment what your approach to buying a house would be. Some of the questions you might ask would focus on its location and how long your commute to work would be, whether it is close to schools, friends, family, etc., whether it is affordable, how much of a mortgage is needed and what kind of mortgage options are available that represent best value. It would be reasonable to assume that you would weigh up your options and your decision would be an informed one, taking into account many factors that will influence which way to go.

Likewise, with separating, we have a responsibility to inform ourselves as well as we can about what is the best approach to take. This is also about becoming aware of what our assets are, and being realistic about how much they are really worth. Many families are in debt – the cost of a lifestyle that may be beyond their means – so they will also need to look at outstanding debts. What are your incomings and outgoings?

Although friends may be well meaning by offering you their advice based on what happened to them or someone they know, please do not be under the illusion that the same will also apply to you.

Seeking professional help – from a mediator, collaborative lawyer or solicitor, etc. – can be daunting as neither of you may know what to expect except what you hear anecdotally. However, if you are getting outside help, it is better to go prepared with a list of questions and have information to hand. It places you in a more powerful personal position than if you know nothing and find yourself saying 'I don't know' in response to their questions. You will only come away more confused and afraid of what's coming next, which is likely to be a more protracted and prolonged (and expensive) legal process than necessary. Some couples take years to finalise their separation because they weren't realistic from the start and their emotions became their driving force, which completely obliterated all common sense and practicality. Maybe this is another reason why working through your grief at this time is so important and why standing back and responding with your head rather than your impulsive feelings can put you on a stronger footing.

The Impact of Formalising Separation

As we go through the process of disentangling our belongings and sorting out what goes to whom, etc., we often forget the impact this has on us as a person. We can drift from one day to another and, finally, when the day arrives to sign a formal agreement, the meaning of it can hit us like a tonne of bricks. Up until this point, for some people anyway, the experience can seem surreal. They may have been drifting along; they know the relationship is over and their partner is gone and may be moving on in their own life. So it may come as some surprise to realise that, once again, you are thrown back into pain as you finally sign on the dotted line. Signing a separation agreement is a defining moment. It might be one that you are dreading or one that you don't really have any thoughts on at all until the time comes.

> Claire (41): 'I got caught up in trying to manage to keep my kids' lives as normal as possible for six months after we decided to separate. I knew I had to get a job in order to have some kind of life where we weren't constantly in debt, so I became busy sending off CVs and attending interviews, when I wasn't clearing out all our stuff to see what was to be divided. To be honest, I didn't really think about what was happening because I was so busy. My husband had left the month before and I was relieved because we had five months of tension in the house up until then. The upside was that during that time we sorted out most of the practical stuff ourselves before we got an agreement drawn up by our mediator.
>
> It was only on the day the agreement was being signed and when I saw my signature going onto it that it dawned on me 'I'm doing this, I'm actually separated. My marriage is over. My old life is gone.' I started trembling at that point, like that feeling you get when someone rear-ends you in a crash. I ran out of the office and couldn't even see in front of me with the tears. I have no idea how I got home but when I got there, I locked myself in my bedroom and cried until it was dark.'

Claire didn't realise the significance for her of signing her separation agreement. She thought it would just be another step in the process, but didn't consider how she'd actually feel. It was impossible for her to know how she would be affected beforehand.

If you are going to be signing something similar, you might think you are being hard done by or be relieved, but you cannot really anticipate the impact it will have on you until it happens. Plan for this. Getting to and from the appointment safely should be a consideration. Can you ask someone close to you to be available, should you need their support?

Sometimes people have an expectation of finality once the agreement has been signed, that somehow all of the stress and upset of separation will be over, only to find that things are exactly the same, nothing's changed and they still feel exactly the same. This can be a low point, especially if you believed that your new life would begin once the agreement was signed. Don't worry; it's only your expectations that have let you down. Like other feelings, this will pass.

As you digest that you are no longer someone's husband or wife, you can begin to ask the questions, 'Who am I now and who do I have the courage to be?'

Chapter 9

Who Am I After Separation?

> Jane (32): 'I felt so empty – no one told me it would feel like this. Have I made a mistake in leaving him? I'm wondering about that now because I feel so bad.'

In the more normal course of events, *physical* separation is a gradual process that takes place at some point after the decision to separate is made. Occasionally, though, the departure of one partner is immediate – no sooner has the news been announced than belongings are gathered up and someone leaves. This can happen in the case of violence, when the need for safety becomes the determining factor in an immediate departure, or when one person in the relationship plans to leave without telling the other until the last minute.

The one who is left behind is in shock and has no time to digest what is happening – they may have had no warning. This sudden type of separation, where there is little or no explanation, often leaves a legacy of unfinished emotional business between you as a couple and can cause disruption to your healing and moving on.

The end of a relationship means a big life change, even if it is something you both finally agree is the best thing for you and/or your family. Loss of a partner has a tendency to bring up powerful feelings of anxiety, sadness, and the fear of being abandoned and being left alone. Rejection, on the other hand, evokes feelings of inadequacy, of having failed somehow, and of shame and humiliation.

In her book *Necessary Losses*, Judith Viorst describes separation as:

> giving rise to anxiety when the loss is either impending or thought to be temporary. Anxiety contains a kernel of hope. But when loss appears to be permanent, anxiety – protest – gives way to depression – despair – and we may not feel lonely and sad but responsible ('I drove her away') and helpless ('I can do nothing to bring her back') and unlovable ('There is something about me that makes me unworthy of love') and hopeless ('Therefore I'll feel this way forever'). (2002, p. 31)

Regardless of how a relationship ends, one of the common experiences to come out of it, for at least a short time anyway, is a loss of confidence. As the other person is now gone from your life, you wonder about yourself. This may affect you in several ways, from how you are performing at work to sexually, socially, and your belief in yourself that you can go it alone and make a new life.

Dominic (46): 'She was always there, a part of me like an arm or a leg. She encouraged and comforted me in every way, a bit like a mother would do. I wasn't a defenceless baby or anything because we were also friends, lovers and parents. She was my life, my comrade-in-arms. And then she was gone .... I begged her to stay but she was determined to leave. For months afterwards, I felt dizzy and confused. I could take care of the everyday things but her not being there was a big hole. She was like a ghost, a presence but not anything I could see or reach out to and touch anymore. I would end up talking to myself in the evenings when I came home, imagining conversations we would have – it sounds like a mad thing to say, but ironically I thought I'd go insane with the silence otherwise.'

Even if it was more of a gradual erosion of the relationship, to finally realise that your relationship is over is akin to discovering that someone you cared about has died. Although death and separation are mourned in similar ways, separation can bring up more anger than a loss through death. Yet the sadness and yearning can be just as intense. The feelings of abandonment when we lose someone we love can be even stronger when they break up with us because they chose to leave.

Sharon (42): 'Even though it was nearly a year before my husband moved out, I was surprised that after the initial "Thank God, finally it's happened" I went back again into the horrible feelings that come with the break-up, the feelings I'd had for nearly two years before he left. My friend had gone through this a few years before and she told me that this would happen, but I was so adamant that there was no way that would be the case with me because I wanted the separation so much. Doubt set in and I become almost obsessed with the idea that it was all a big mistake and that we really should be together after all. I approached him about it. He got really mad with me, saying how dare I put him through all this and now say I wanted him back. To be honest, it hurt – his rejection nearly sent me over the edge. For a while I believed the pain I felt at him pushing me away was because I really did love him and wanted the relationship back on again. But my friend was adamant it was just the grief I was feeling because everything was different now.'

153

It is natural to expect that the turmoil we experience in the lead up to a physical separation will quieten down once it is finally over, only to find that we are feeling at odds with our reality now. It is entirely natural for you to go back into grieving if you find yourself in this position. It is not quite what I would describe as a vapour trail or the tail end of your relationship because the feelings that are experienced at this stage can be very intense. You had something unique with your partner, even if there was much unhappiness between you. You are bound to feel that hole that Sharon remembers or the almost ethereal presence that Dominic describes. Not only has the other person now gone, but your everyday life is different without them – you haven't just lost that person but everything they represented for you.

Relationships develop from needs: the need to be loved; the need to belong; the need to take care of someone else or to be taken care of ourselves. For many, having a partner means that you have someone with whom you can share the joy of having children, and with whom you can hopefully enjoy increased financial security. Our identities become enmeshed in our relationship. Our partner and, consequently, the relationship give us a sense of belonging, a place in the world. However, when that relationship is gone, when we are no longer part of a 'we', a period of adjustment takes place as we try to get used to our new life without them. We enter into a zone where we're not quite dead, but nor do we feel the vitality of life. It's an in-between space that a physical separation places us in and it does take some getting used to. Some aspects of this situation might be better than when you were together with your ex, and some might be worse.

Many will say that they are getting on with their lives, picking up the pieces and getting used to not being with their partner anymore. But small things like filling in an application form can bring up the pain of loss all over again. In the 'marital status' column of application forms we declare our relationship status, and we are reminded once more of what has happened to our relationship. If you are female and were married, you might ask yourself, 'What do I sign my name as? Ms? Mrs? Miss? Do I now put down my maiden name? Who am I anyway?' As mentioned in an earlier chapter, even sending greeting cards and leaving one person's name out can be upsetting, and can also bring up anger and hurt.

The entire journey of separation can be experienced as if you are creeping along. It may appear as if you are making great strides in terms of healing and moving ahead, but you can hit a brick wall at any point and despair that you will ever come out at the other end. Have faith. We experience loss from the moment we are born – loss of the precious room we inhabited in our mother's womb. We become more resilient along the way and develop a style of coping with each loss on our developmental journey. What we are experiencing now is another loss, and a major one, entirely different to losing a possession such as a set of keys. Our partner played many roles for us and we for them. Even if our confidence is now at low ebb, the challenge becomes one of re-building our lives without our former partners and in a new set of circumstances.

Although some people leave a relationship to start a new one, most will be on their own for a while at least. They are now single, perhaps for the first time. If a person does not have a strong sense of themselves going into that relationship or else found that their individual identity disappeared over time in that relationship, it may seem impossible for them to imagine that they could ever pick up the pieces and be happy again. Although people do experience distance from their partners in relationships and loneliness may be a constant companion, to finally be on your own can be isolating and frightening and we can feel a deep emptiness inside. Separation is not easy for anyone, but it is even more difficult for the person who is used to being in a relationship and who doesn't like being out of one. They don't necessarily feel comfortable with themselves, even if they have been tending to the needs of others all their lives and welcome the idea that they now have more time for themselves and for doing as they please. This jars somehow with their identity and will take a bit of time to get used to. On one level, they may enjoy the freedom of being single, yet they miss the hurly burly of their old life and feel acutely the space that was once occupied by their partner.

Even the change to mundane routines can affect a person at this time. Where once there was someone to greet 'hello' to when you walked through the door in the evening, there may now be only silence punctuated by the ticking of a clock. Perhaps you have moved to a new home and feel a kind of awkwardness being there – you are not quite used to it yet. If you have stayed in the home where you both lived together, it can seem too big and empty, like something large is missing.

> Joanna (51): 'I could still smell him and would almost be expecting him through the door in the evening. I kept imagining his head popping around the door and asking me if I fancied a cuppa. I found myself sleeping on his side of the bed, trying desperately to hold onto what once was, but inevitably would end up sobbing. In the initial weeks, there were many nights when I couldn't sleep and would pace the floor for hours while the rest of the world slept. I felt like someone had ripped off one of my limbs. I didn't want to live anymore.'

In an effort to maintain somewhat of a connection with their ex-partner, some people will wonder over and over about what their ex-partner is doing and will want to stay in constant touch, simply because they miss their partner and their life together. While this is natural – after all, you have been together a long time and may have invested heavily in that relationship – it does distract you from yourself in the present. Your attention is still on your ex-partner and you are still investing emotionally in that relationship. If you find yourself doing this, try to distract yourself by doing something else, whether it is going out with a friend or completing a task that will give you a sense of achievement such as mowing the lawn, cleaning or painting, etc. Although it might seem like you have to force yourself out of wallowing (which can become a habit that is hard to break), you have enough on your plate without adding the burden of constant self-pity to the load. Doing positive things for yourself helps to alter unhelpful thinking and rebuilds confidence and self-esteem.

Whatever the nature of the ending, life can feel very strange for quite a while. As time moves on after the physical separation, you might still be feeling in a bit of a jumble – one day you're up and the next day you're right back in a very painful place. Even if you were the one who wanted to end the relationship, you can find yourself questioning whether you made the right decision. You may start thinking of your former partner in a new light or may miss some of the little things they did that you liked. If your partner was the one who left you, it can be just as confusing. You might wonder what you could have done to make a difference. Even worse, you could blame yourself entirely for the ending.

To continue to have strong feelings for your ex-partner is natural, even long after a physical separation. Feelings don't just stop when you finally say goodbye. For people who have had children together, for example, they will hopefully continue to keep some sort of bond in place. It is now a parenting bond, quite separate from a couple bond. When you catch sight of each other, at handover times, for instance, it can be enough to bring all the pain and hurt back again. However, feelings do change over time.

There may still be an expectation that your ex-partner will do what they say they will do and when they say they will do it, especially in relation to children; yet, somehow they let you down. This may be a continuance of the pattern that was in your relationship when you were a couple and, even though you are now no longer together, they still have the ability to upset you when they fail to come through with their

157

promises. For some, it can feel like the burden of childrearing is left to them if their ex is not willing to share the load. Others may be hoping to see the children and then their ex-partner decides otherwise. This can be very depressing and can make them feel as if they do not have any say or sway on parenting issues.

If you are living away from the family home and start noticing that the children don't want to talk to or see you, you may wonder if your ex-partner is trying to turn them against you. If you are the custodial parent, the children may seem very well-behaved when they are with your ex-partner and yet they are like demons to live with. Perhaps they take time to settle back in with you after a visit to the other parent. No matter whether you are the custodial parent or not, you may see your ex-partner as having the preferred parental role.

Dealing with Feelings of Abandonment

Abandonment is a word used to describe a feeling or experience of separateness – you can either feel it emotionally or be physically abandoned, or both. It is, however, linked to dependency on another. Let's look at co-dependency for a moment. Its definition has been developed over the years and one particular version I like is Melody Beattie's, who explains it as 'one who has let another person's behaviour affect him or her, and who is obsessed with controlling that person's behaviour'. She believes that

> the heart of the definition ... lies not in the other person – no matter how much we believe it does. It lies in ourselves, in the ways we have let other people's behaviour affect us and in the ways we try to affect them: the obsessing, the controlling, the obsessive 'helping' caretaking, low self-worth bordering on self-hatred, self-repression, abundance of anger and guilt, peculiar dependency on peculiar people, attraction to and tolerance for the

bizarre, other-centeredness that results in abandonment of self, communication problems, intimacy problems .... (1992, p. 36)

Stepping away from the connection or dependency we have on another can seem impossible if we are still caught up in the old relationship. Perhaps it is the only way we know how to be. We may not yet know how to do things differently or maybe we feel lacking in the courage that is required to change. We behave in ways to deal with our abandonment by clinging to our ex-partner or our children so we don't feel so utterly alone.

Alternatively we can pretend that everything is okay and we are managing well – it's the mask we wear (even for ourselves) to conceal pain and prevent us from falling apart. We believe we have the strength to survive the loss. We don't mean to do it, but it becomes our style of coping. Another way of dealing with such a loss is to swing back and forth between yearning and distancing – very confusing altogether.

Inside all of us is the struggle to deal with the humiliation and shame that comes with an irrevocably failed relationship and to restore a sense of pride in an attempt to prove that we are good enough. We can blame our partner for what went wrong so that we remain intact as good people. When our partner leaves us, it can feel like an attack, like we've done something horribly wrong. We feel as if we've been betrayed and exploited and, in extreme cases, we even develop a sense of feeling conspired against. When this happens, we begin to remember our ex-partner as being a devious, horrible person and not the one we fell in love with, and we may wonder if we were being 'set up' all along. However, it is important to remember that this relationship gave you meaning and purpose at the time. You entered into it with the hope that your love would be everlasting and reciprocated, and now you are faced with the reality that this did not, in fact, happen. You can make a fresh start without denying what was good or bad in that relationship; in fact, to deny the good in the relationship and pretend it wasn't worth anything is like brushing away the good in yourself, and the great aspects you and your partner brought to it that made it worth something, even if it no longer exists. These aspects taught you what the feelings of love are really about. No one would have stayed in a relationship if it didn't work on some level, even if there were only fleeting blissful moments. These moments are what gave us hope to keep going. It's the other less desirable aspects that caused it to fail. Hold on to the good if you can, not in a way that causes you to yearn for the old relationship but to give you hope that you can re-create it again, firstly with yourself (and build confidence and self-value) and then in a new relationship when you think you're ready.

It's important to take good care of ourselves, emotionally, physically, practically and spiritually, during this period of transition and loss. We should find the support we need and learn to be compassionate with ourselves (and by that I mean to just be accepting of our very difficult and often uncomfortable feelings), so we can heal.

You and Your Home

If you are the one who moves out, you may be staying in temporary accommodation at your parents' or child's home or with a friend or sibling. Or you may end up renting somewhere if you can afford it until the dust has settled. Physical separation does have a financial impact one way or the other and this can bring an added burden of worry about trying to make ends meet if you are still supporting your ex-partner and/or children or if your ex-partner was the main or sole breadwinner. It can also be quite lonely being apart, even if things weren't going well between you before separating. Your new home may have no personal stamp on it yet. If this is important to you, try to make sure that at least some of the things you treasure and like are visible around you to help you settle in. Having something familiar around you can be comforting. That's why small children carry toys with them wherever they go. It helps them to feel safe and secure. I'm not suggesting that you act like a child, but there is a great deal of common sense to holding onto some things from your old life to help you along.

If you are the one staying put, there may be lots of reminders in your home of your relationship. It can be difficult to motivate yourself to get rid of your ex-partner's belongings or remnants of your life together. And, perhaps for the moment, you can't begin a big clearout. However, research has shown that simple things like painting a wall or planting something new in your garden does have a therapeutic effect, bringing a shift or change, even just a small one. Creating something new while holding onto something old is actually a form of moving on. This can help you until such time as you find yourself chucking something away from your old life, or giving an old belonging to someone who may have better use for it. Some people find that moving furniture around can have a cathartic effect. You can always move it back if it doesn't look right.

Friends

As mentioned, an unfortunate side effect of separation is that you may lose some friends as a result. You may also find yourself at the centre of gossip which can be hurtful and unjust. It can be surprising to discover that some friends will side with your ex. This can give rise to anger and annoyance that they have picked your ex over you, and you may wonder what's behind it. It's okay to be hurt about it and to feel betrayed by them. However, this is yet another loss and is symptomatic of the ending of your relationship.

People who have friends who are separating often don't know how to continue to be friends with both of you and may feel coerced into taking sides. It's awkward and uncomfortable for them and they are at a loss to know what to do about it. They may even decide that the best thing for them is to retreat from both of you. If their own relationship is struggling and they're not feeling secure about their partner for whatever reason, they could see your separation as a threat. Many articles have been written about how single women will often be seen as a threat to women who are in relationships. The sad thing is that, even if she isn't the least bit attracted to the man or men in question, she can still be rejected as a result. By contrast, the newly single man is more likely to be seen as a welcome addition to a dinner party or social outing.

Being newly separated also means that you are free to socialise as you wish, because you are now single and available. Even if you do not yet feel ready to meet someone new, you may want your friends to join you on nights out as a way to occupy your free time. Such friends may be in a different position to you and may have obligations or commitments at home, so they may not be interested in trying new things or going to new places which, although beneficial to you, don't really fit into their lives, not on a regular basis anyway. They may also resent your freedom to be with anyone you want whilst they are 'trapped' at home. You now have less in common with them and the bond of friendship may start to loosen and the friendship falls away.

Believe it or not, it is probably best that some friendships end; anyway, it's impossible to hold on to everyone from your old life. But it can be painful to let go when you really want to hold on. In any event, it is highly likely that with a new life comes new friends, ones you pick on your own and who are more suited to your personality and needs.

The Plan for Your New Life

Although you might not be at all happy being on your own after separation, it is now a perfect opportunity to look at what is in your life at present, what is still useful to you, what you need to let go of and what you might like to attract into your life that will make you happy. Outlined below are some ideas to get you started. These are well-known tools used by life coaches, counsellors and other professionals whose job is focused on helping people who want to make a meaningful change in their lives.

Values

Values give us a sense of purpose, a measure of what's important to us in our lives. The closer we live in alignment with our values, the more we are likely to feel balanced and happy. If you believe that you value being with your family and yet you are never with them, then too much time away from them will make you unhappy and at odds with yourself until you change your circumstances.

Conversely, if you know that exercise is something you value and you actually fit in time to exercise on a regular basis you are more likely to be happy in yourself if you are honouring that value. On a basic level, you are honouring a need in yourself.

If you have never actually sat down and thought about what your values are, why not do it now? The benefit of doing something like this is that we become more in touch with who we are, what matters most to us and what is important for us to have in our lives. Separating may not have been something you wanted and you might be still missing your old life with your ex, but at some point, and maybe reluctantly, you will have to start re-claiming parts of yourself as an individual.

Here are some examples to begin with. You may have other values that you'd like to add and please feel free to do so because this is about what matters to *you*. Please note that money is not a value – it's only a currency to provide a particular lifestyle. If you are yearning for your old relationship, rather than putting your ex in there, perhaps think about the qualities that are important to you in a relationship.

What Are Your Values?

Achievement	Fast living	Physical challenge
Advancement and promotion	Freedom	Pleasure
Adventure	Friendships	Power and authority
Affection (love and caring)	Growth	Privacy
Arts	Having a family	Public service
Being around people who are open and honest	Helping other people	Purity
Challenging problems	Helping society	Quality relationships
Change and variety	Honesty	Recognition (respect from others, status)
Close relationships	Independence	Religion
Community	Influencing others	Reputation
Competence	Inner harmony	Responsibility and accountability
Competition	Integrity	Security
Cooperation	Intellectual status	Self-respect
Country	Involvement	Serenity
Creativity	Job tranquility	Sophistication
Decisiveness	Knowledge	Stability
Democracy	Leadership	Status
Ecological awareness	Location	Supervising others
Economic security	Loyalty	Taking part in things
Effectiveness	Market position	Time freedom
Efficiency	Meaningful work	Wealth
Ethical practice	Merit	Wisdom
Excellence	Nature	Work under pressure
Excitement	Order (tranqulity, stability, conformity)	Work with others
Fame	Personal development	Working alone

Adapted from www.selfcounseling.com

From your list, please select the top ten values that you feel have most meaning for you. Imagine that you are only permitted to have five values. Which five would you give up? Cross them off. Now imagine that you are only permitted four. Which would you give up? Cross it off. Now cross off another, to bring your list down to three.

Ask yourself if you are living in accordance with these values as much as you can, or is there something you can do to align yourself more closely with your key values? Are there other values that are aspirational and you feel would be good to live by in your new life? What can you do about making them part of you?

The Law of Attraction

Most people have heard of the Law of Attraction, which is based on the principle of 'like attracting like'. Essentially, your thoughts have the power to attract certain things into your life; what you think about and thank about, you bring about! In even simpler terms, what you give your focus and attention to will be what you manifest, whether it is something you want or you don't want. So, if you're feeling confused, your life may be reflecting this: the house may seem chaotic and nothing is in its proper place; at work you may find it difficult to finish projects and to plan ahead. Generally, it might seem that people are letting you down and you feel excluded. In the midst of all this confusion, we need to start, sooner or later, to turn it around and become clearer about what we want and start taking steps in that direction. These may only be small steps at first, and that's perfectly okay because they're steps towards developing positive habits in your new life.

Your new life will take many twists and turns, just like your old life did. Yet, there may be some things that will remain the same as before because it is not possible to change them at present or because they are still useful to you. However, the things you want to change are worth exploring. Illustrated below is a sample of a tool called the Wheel of Life which is used by life

coaches, counselling therapists and other people who help individuals who are trying to make some change in their lives. It is a
simple chart designed to provide you with an overview of your
life and see where might be the easiest place to start.

Copy the wheel down on a blank piece of paper. There are
twelve significant aspects of life mentioned, although there
may be other dimensions that have more meaning for you
and, if that is the case, use them instead. Shade in, from the
centre outwards, your level of satisfaction with each area. For
example, you might love your job and not really be able to find
it lacking in any way. So you might shade in most, if not the
entire, area allocated to that part of your life. On the other hand,
perhaps relationships aren't so good at the moment and you
feel that this section only merits being shaded in about a third.
Keep going until all the areas have been shaded according to
how satisfied you are with each. Then imagine or visualise each
section being fully shaded and what might have changed to
allow this to be the case.

Figure 1: The Wheel of Life

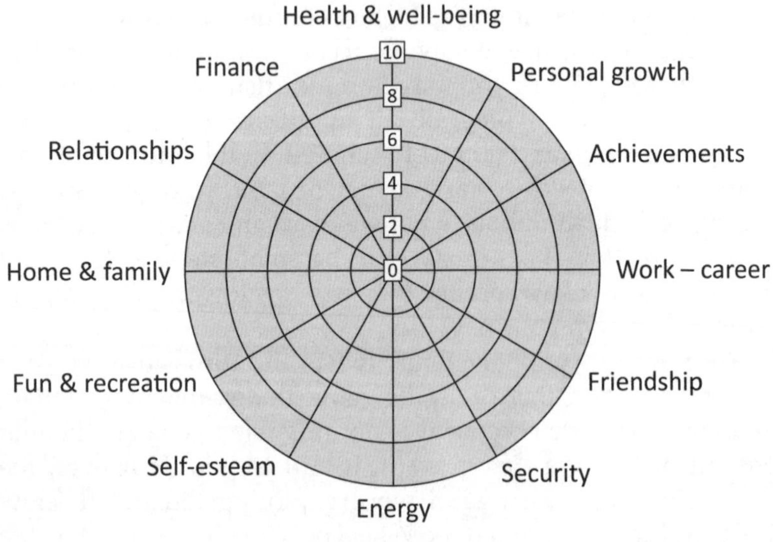

As you look at the wheel now, assess how balanced it is overall. If it was a wheel on your bike, would it be a bumpy ride or not? Are you giving more time and attention to one or two particular areas? Is it frustrating or satisfying? Do you need to give more to one aspect of your life and less to another at the moment? The overall aim is to balance out your life as much as possible and also to find ways to improve the quality of your overall happiness.

Taking the example of fun and recreation, if you cannot shade it in enough to your satisfaction and want more of it in your life, pause and, using the Law of Attraction, focus on the following:

- Imagine you are having fun. Where would you be? What would you be doing? Who would you be with? How are you feeling? What is your body sense (are you relaxed, excited or both)?

- What kind of people bring out the best in you? What do you do to bring out the best in yourself so that you are fun to be around?

- What can you do to make this happen? Is there any way you can close the gap so that you can have a bit more fun right now?

Really try to imagine how you would feel if you were having fun. Write it down in the present tense and that way you are sending a *clear* signal to yourself of what you want. This is what you will attract into your life. Be clear about what you want and visualise it (and use your emotions to feel it). Leave any 'buts' and replace them with 'ands' so that you keep your intentions clear and your mindset positive.

For example: 'I'm with X. We are laughing a lot and chatting away, really enjoying each other's company. We enjoy the same activities and we're off doing things with each other. I'm smiling a lot and feel relaxed. I notice X likes my company and the banter is easy between us.'

This is what's called an affirmation – affirmations are statements that use positive language and avoid stating what you *don't* want. The most important part of visualising this has to do with *feelings*, so really try to feel your emotion as if you're experiencing it in the here and now. The lovely thing about visualising what you want is that you may now have the opportunity to bring this into your life, which may not have been possible while you were in your old relationship.

In addition, as you go to bed at night, think of five things you have in your life that you are grateful for – this works on your subconscious as you sleep and helps to manifest a positive mindset. Try to make it a different five things each night because this requires your brain to recall the daily memories with conscious or mindful attention and reinforces positive thinking.

Gerry (44): 'I fell apart for a while; my misery just engulfed me. It seemed hopeless – stuck in that black hole, in complete darkness with no stepladder out of there. I was on anti-depressants but I knew they would only take the edge off it. The weekends when I didn't have my kids were the worst. I used to be sporty when I was younger but I became very unfit and overweight over the years. After my separation, I was broke and could only afford a few cans of beer in the week at home and on my own. Looking back now, I can see that I was acting like a saddo, whinging to anyone who'd listen to me and secretly hating myself although I wouldn't admit my loneliness to anyone. I was the big guy who was full of laughs and happy in himself. One of the girls at work noticed I was different, that I wasn't the same as before. I don't know whether she was doing it out of sympathy or whether she needed the company, but she asked me would I walk with her some evening because she was trying to lose weight and was finding it hard to stay motivated on her own. I said no at first because I wasn't great company and I was looking forward to the couch. But as I threw myself on the couch later, I realised that it was one more night doing the same old thing and, frankly, I was bored. So I texted her and we walked for two miles that evening.

Coming back into the house after, it was hard to ignore that I felt a tiny bit better. Even though the exercise was hard (she was small but quick) I felt like I'd been injected with something and, for the first time in ages, I fell asleep quickly. The next evening it was sunny and we did it again, and pretty quickly we were walking for five miles a few times a week. We laughed about things that happened during the day at work. I told her about how hard things were for me personally but she didn't seem surprised. The best bit was that I started to lose weight and my big concern now was being able to afford to buy new clothes. As the soccer season started again, I began to look around and see if I could play a bit of 5-a-side or 7-a-side or join my old club where I could train and maybe get a few games with one of the reserve teams.

One of the lads on the team I ended up playing on had a sister who I liked. I would never have had the confidence to ask her out a few months before that but all I could think of was the worst thing she could say was no and maybe she'd be flattered I'd asked her anyway. She said yes and now we've been going out together for a year. I am now nearly three stone lighter, a lot happier and have a great woman in my life and all because I said yes to a walk.'

The above suggestions are simple, tried-and-tested methods for opening a person up to the possibility that they can have a good and happy life in the future. Right now, life may not seem so good and it can be hard to have hope. Your path has changed and you will have changed too. However, there are some things where you have choice. You are standing at a metaphorical crossroads and you can choose your path for the future. 'How will you seize the moment? No one else can dance your dance, no one else can sing your song, no one else can write your story. Who you are, what you do, begins right now!' (Byrne 2006, p. 182)

sense of anticipative anxiety and it can come across to others as quite controlling. In any event, we'll never really know whether we were loved in a relationship because we manipulated a situation or influenced our partner to give us the outcome we desired, or because they loved us enough anyway.

In an ideal world, we would always value ourselves for who we are and not what we do. We would continuously live our lives in an open, honest and relaxed manner and that includes being able to always state our needs, thus building strong levels of self-esteem.

In their book *Rebuilding – When Your Relationship Ends*, Bruce Fisher and Robert Alberti explore the notion of falling in love by describing it as the:

> warm fuzzies with a fish hook in them. A 'warm fuzzy' is a nice gesture that you give somebody – such as saying 'I love you'. Unfortunately, many of us are still struggling to fulfil *ourselves*. If your own life bucket is nearly empty when you say, 'I love you' to another person, it probably means, 'Please love me'. The other person finds the warm fuzzy, swallows it and is hooked. Saying 'I love you' from an empty bucket tends to be manipulative, while love from a full bucket allows others to be themselves and to be free.
>
> Another problem with love in our society is that falling in love is the most acceptable reason for getting married. However 'falling in love' may have more to do with lone-liness than with warmth towards the other person. Falling in love to overcome loneliness is not actually love. It is rather a feeling of warmth which comes from breaking down the barriers that have kept us from being intimate with other people.
>
> Sometimes one does not love the other person, but loves instead the idealized image of that person. When the dif-ference is realised, one becomes disillusioned, falls out of love, and the relationship is dissolved. (2006, p. 178)

Relationships that start so soon after a separation tend to be transitory because they are not really based on getting to know someone over time and falling in love with that person and because you appreciate and enjoy each other. There's intensity to some of these transitional relationships, a kind of neediness that fuels excitement and passion. Perhaps it makes you feel alive after what you've been through, but bear in mind that the more you invest in this second relationship at such an early stage, the more devastated and despairing you are likely to become if it doesn't work out. So, please, for yourself, take your time and pace yourself. Enjoy meeting new people and if you find yourself becoming either romantically or sexually involved with someone, remember that you are vulnerable at the moment. Although it is exciting to meet someone who you think could be special, you still need to take care of yourself.

Loving Me

Growing up with a healthy sense of self means not just relying on others to tell us that we are good enough, but, as we mature, hopefully developing an internal sense of self-approval. Hence, we do not rely *only* on what others say, but we have a well-established inner sense of our own goodness – what comes from the outside matches how we feel on the inside. All information is neutral until we process it through our personal filters. How we digest it is based primarily on our previous experiences which inform us how to think, feel and behave. That's why two people can have different experiences of the same thing. If we are prone to negative thinking, it is unlikely that we will take a positive meaning from something someone has said about us or to us. How we receive compliments is a simple example. Below are two different scenarios of how people can respond to a compliment.

Negative:

Other: You look well today.

Me: Are you joking me? I look like a fright. I haven't washed my hair in a week.

Other: Well, I think you're looking well but sorry you think otherwise.

The person who paid the compliment may now feel foolish or insulted for saying anything in the first place. They may be slow to compliment you again in the future. If there are fewer compliments coming your way, this may reinforce a belief that you aren't attractive. Because you are thinking negatively you aren't allowing the nice stuff to come in.

Positive:

Other: You look well today.

Me: Ah, thanks. I'm feeling quite good actually.

or

         It's nice to hear that because I don't really know how I feel today. Thanks!

Other: Ah, good!

The other person is likely to be smiling. You're likely to be smiling. You are both giving off positive energy to each other and are likely to connect better in the conversation that follows. The other person is also likely to compliment you again in the future, knowing it will be a good experience for them too.

Which scenario would you prefer to be part of?

It is so common in the aftermath of separation to find yourself at a low ebb – your self-esteem might be compromised and your self-confidence (what you believe in terms of your abilities) may be rather wobbly. Although you may have come out of a failed relationship, this does not mean you are a failure. Even if you have doubts about whether you are lovable or whether you have the ability to fall in love again, one of the big goals after separation is to learn to accept and love yourself as you are today. This might sound a bit 'soft'. It may not appeal to those people who prefer to invest their love in other people. Their love has always been projected outwards to another person, and when they separate from that person the loss they feel is devastating: who will they shower all their love on now? Unconsciously, the person who gives all their love to others but not to themselves may be echoing a much deeper need, which is to be loved themselves, as described by Fisher and Alberti earlier in the chapter. When love doesn't come back to them in a way that is recognised, they are left with disappointment and perhaps a message that they aren't that lovable after all. There is nothing wrong with loving yourself. It is quite different to narcissism, which is all about 'me, me, me'. To love yourself means that you respect yourself, you pay attention to your feelings and you act in a way that gives you a strong message that you matter. Give yourself the respect and latitude to be yourself rather than to be what others want or expect you to be.

Knowing Your Shadow Side

No one, on a conscious level anyway, likes admitting they have a shadow side: that part of us we hide from others because we fear they will reject us. Somehow we have picked up a message along the way that some aspect of ourselves is unacceptable or we have a certain trait or feeling that is hard to admit to. We then tuck it out of the way, out of sight, even from ourselves. Our shadow side is shown to us when we have a strong feeling or reaction to what others say and do. For example, if we have a generous, giving nature but have a tendency to over-give, we may find it hard when another person (who might also be generous and giving) says 'No'. We might feel distinctly uncomfortable, perhaps resentful and feel rejected by them. People who find it hard to say 'No' and find themselves saying 'Yes' to something when they really don't want to are avoiding rejection. What they see in the other person are personal boundaries (or limits) that they have yet to develop themselves.

In reality, a person with strong *flexible* boundaries will recognise that they can say 'Yes' and 'No' without guilt or remorse – they weigh up a situation that requires a yes or no response and consider their own personal needs as well as those of others. Another way to recognise your shadow side is when you say one thing and do another – your action is coming from your shadow or unconscious side. For example, you might say you want a happy, healthy relationship and yet you have relationships that tend to make you very unhappy and anxious. This is when your shadow comes out to play. Perhaps within its murky depths is a belief that you don't deserve a good relationship or that perhaps you have little trust in a relationship working out. It's good to know what emotions and problems you are carrying with you and a good counsellor can help you with this. When we can see what's behind our shadow side, it usually loses its power over us and we become more balanced and in control as a person. Our shadow side also notes the good things that other people have but that we think we don't possess. Ergo, we paint ourselves in a poor light and unjustifiably so – a good rule of thumb is that 'we only know what we recognise and we only recognise what we know', that is, you will not recognise or identify with something if it is not part of you already.

Ironically, it is only by accepting our dark or shadow side that we 'become' our potential. Other people will often be aware of our shadow side anyway, even if it is out of our awareness.

Michael (45): 'I had been separated for six years and was in and out of casual relationships since then. Although I really wanted to find a new partner, I seemed to sabotage every chance at a relationship and it seemed that the only women who were in my life wanted a casual and uncommitted relationship. My ex-wife had hurt me quite badly by having an affair and I didn't want to stay in our marriage after that. I didn't want anyone to see how it affected me, so I kept a brave face and got on with my life. I never let myself get sad or down – what was the point? Being the life and soul of the party became an important part of my persona – I'd been like that from an early age because there was illness and depression in my family and someone needed to be the one who stayed 'up'. It was a role very familiar to me as I didn't want to turn out like either of my parents.

Heading into my forties wasn't something I looked forward to on my own – I remember feeling desperate and a bit panicky, unsettled. I didn't really know what was wrong but definitely knew something wasn't right. The bottom line was I wanted a new relationship, yet I was terrified to risk it. Last year, a work colleague put me in touch with a good counsellor. I was initially sceptical but knew that it couldn't be any worse than where I was at that point.

As I trawled through what had happened to my marriage with the counsellor, it became obvious that because I was so focused on maintaining my own sense of pride and didn't want to admit any weakness or to being a victim of what had happened I had been acting from that fear. The counsellor questioned whether my shadow side was running the show, the bit of me that I wanted to run as far away as possible from. I wouldn't let anyone see me vulnerable, but, paradoxically, the hurt and sadness in a way kept me stuck as a victim ever since. Being hurt and sad about what had happened was a very difficult thing to admit to anyone but, strangely enough, it was also a relief.

A few months later, I met a girl. I am really enjoying being with her and we're taking it slowly. There are moments when I feel we are getting closer – before this I used to 'disappear' if I felt I was falling for someone , but it doesn't freak me out as much anymore, as I am much more relaxed and in control without even trying. It's nice!'

Michael had recognised that something wasn't quite right and he couldn't get to the bottom of it by himself. What he learned by facing his shadow side permitted him to accept himself and his vulnerability, which he'd been denying. He seemed to naturally become more secure within himself. Even just admitting it to someone else provided a release from the power that it seemed to have over him, which had limited his ability to start any meaningful relationship.

When you accept yourself as you are, both the good and the bad, then you are in a position to become more like the person you want to be. To be fair, most of us may not even know we have this shadow side to ourselves because it's buried in our unconscious and it may only be the fear of the pain we believe we will experience that stops us from becoming curious. It is more than likely that with a bit of help (and counselling is a safe way to do this) to face our shadow side, the worst we'll feel is an intensity of emotion for a short while, which will quickly subside. Like Michael, calm will settle in as we digest and absorb the information. We no longer fear this side of ourselves; we just begin to accept it as part of who we are.

Fear is a crippling block to success. If you are looking to meet someone new and begin again, don't you think it's worth having a look at who you are in relationships and what you carry with you that can both enhance and limit your future happiness? Some common fears are:

1. Fear of taking a risk

2. Inability to trust

3. Insecurity

4. Fear of being vulnerable

5. Fear of failure

6. Need for approval

7. Fear of rejection

8. Inability to identify feelings

9. Inability to forgive yourself

10. Inability to establish intimacy

(Adapted from: www.livestrong.com.)

How to Start Loving Me

The self-loving concept might feel uncomfortable to start off with. However, there are some ways to kick-start the process, which are listed below. As you settle yourself into the hot seat of feeling good about yourself, remember that, even if you have been through the worst of separations, you are still a person of worth.

Take a pen and paper and (1) *make a list of the things you like about yourself.* Leave out any 'buts' (because they negate what is being said) and put in 'because': for example, rather than saying, 'I like the way I am generous *but* sometimes I feel like I'm taken for granted', instead consider writing, 'I like the way I am generous *because* I feel good being able to help other people.' Needless to say, as you become more respectful of your feelings, they will inform you of when you are over-giving, that is, you will feel like saying no rather than yes. You will become more aware of your discomfort as you put someone else's needs continuously before your own. 'No' is not a dirty word, nor does it mean you are selfish. If we don't say no to others sometimes, it means we are saying no to ourselves always, thereby diminishing our self-esteem and the value of our 'Yes'.

Listing these things that you admire about yourself is about focusing on your positive characteristics and staying positive.

Next, before you go to bed at night, (2) *list at least three things you did that day that you are proud of.* When we do things that we are proud of, we give ourselves a boost and it increases our self-esteem.

(3) *When someone praises you, be sure to say 'Thank you.'* Even if it is uncomfortable at first and you don't really believe them, acknowledge it anyway.

(4) *Be compassionate with yourself when you make a mistake.* We all make them, though sometimes we don't like to admit being in the wrong. But we can be left with a deep sense of upset that can linger, unless we somehow learn to comfort and reassure ourselves that we'll be okay. Rather than justifying our words or actions that caused the mistake to happen, can we accept that it happened and forgive ourselves? People who are compassionate with themselves often find it easier to apologise (if that's what is needed) without losing any self-respect, and the situation resolves itself with no lasting negative effects.

Finally, (5) *have the courage and strength to love yourself.* You've been through a lot and have survived, even if you sometimes wonder how you did. That, in itself, is a testament of your own strength and resilience.

What Do You Want from a New Relationship?

With at least one significant relationship behind you, it is always a good idea to explore what you are about – not only what you want, but why you want it. Knowing and understanding your motivations and desires for wanting a relationship are probably the most important steps towards your own personal happiness, especially if you feel you are ready to meet someone new. Although we all have expectations, and some of them are fantasy that may never bear fruit, at least we can identify what is realistic and what is not. This will be a key factor in attracting the right person and developing a relationship that will enhance you as a person. It will help you to avoid making your new partner responsible for determining whether you are happy or not. If we place a burden on them by being unrealistic, we can mistakenly make the assumption that they are somehow to blame for our frustration and disappointment, and the potential for a lovely new relationship suffers. Based on my own experience of working with couples in second relationships, difficulties are primarily based on unrealistic expectations, confused roles and the presence of children from an earlier relationship, as well as there being less money second time around and continued contact with the first family (including in-laws, etc). A point to note – the incidence of second marriage break-ups in the UK and the US is relatively high (over 50 per cent), compared to that of first marriages.

Expectations are often a giant stumbling block to our personal happiness. Not only do unrealistic expectations cause problems, but dysfunctional ways of dealing with conflict breeds disharmony from one failed relationship to the other. In other words, if I don't correct the dysfunctional approach I take to resolving issues of conflict, then every new relationship has the potential to end up the same as the previous one. For example, if a couple has a style of continuously sweeping difficulties under the carpet and ignoring whatever's there, the issue or issues between them will start to pile up, and over time they will notice that these problems have now formed a wall between them and they can no longer see, hear or get a sense of each other. Even if you want to do it differently next time, unless you learn to communicate and do it with a degree of confidence and respect for yourself and them, there is an increased likelihood that this pattern will be repeated in the next relationship, and on it goes. Don't rely on your new partner to do the work for you.

Being clear and realistic about what you want and being comfortable with that will not come across as being demanding or needy, even if you are accused of that. It may be your partner's way of saying, 'Please don't make me responsible for your feelings of frustration or disappointment.'

A simple way to start exploring what you want from a new relationship is to develop a clear understanding of the following, based on your last or earlier relationship(s). Think back to the start of the relationship(s) and answer the following questions:

What did I think my role would be?
I thought I'd be the one who…
I ended up being the one who…
What did I think was my ex-partner's role?
I wanted them to be…
They turned out to be…

What did I want that relationship to give me?
I wanted the relationship to...
It actually gave me...
In a new relationship, what would I like my role to be?
I'd like to be the one who...
I'd like my partner's role to be...
What qualities would I like to have in my new relationship?
(Remember to be realistic – no relationship will give you every-thing you wish but if you are aware of what you do want, it'll be easier to find it.)
Must have...
Nice to have (but not a deal-breaker)...
As I do this exercise, what do I feel and think right now?
I feel...
I think...

When you meet someone and there seems to be a strong chem-istry, it can be dangerous to attach too much meaning to it. Yes, it might be very exciting to feel that bond with someone else and perhaps we get a glimmer of hope that possibly, just possibly, this is someone special. Instead of feeling flat as we have been, this person somehow injects new life into us and we become sparkly again. This chemistry can feel quite magi-cal, yet all it's telling you is that you're opening yourself up to taking a risk again, not because of someone else, but because you have allowed it.

Wanting a relationship too quickly is likely to breed mistrust and wariness in a new 'love interest'. If this love interest has a grounded sense of themselves, they will quickly become suspicious of you and subsequently become more distant and unavailable. After all, why would you want to get seri-ous before you even had a chance to get to know them first? It screams, 'I need a relationship and I'm not too fussy about who I have it with – I just don't want to be on my own.' The other person will feel the pressure to make you happy and responsi-bility is no fun.

If you are looking for a relationship, why not have it based on something that is built on you both liking each other for who you are, rather than just about getting your needs met – mutual appreciation and genuine affection for each other will sustain your new relationship when the initial heady excitement has worn off.

The better you know your own needs and motivations for wanting to be in a new relationship, the easier it will be for you when it comes to dating.

The Dating Game

It would seem a logical next step to start dating. Lots of people nowadays date because they want to meet new people and have fun without it becoming something serious. The dating scene now, compared to a decade (or more) ago, is quite different. The world today is much more accessible compared to 'back then' when the only people we had access to, realistically, were those with whom we came into contact at work, family, friends, socially and through other people. With the advent of technology, the world of dating has become a much broader arena and online dating, speed dating, personal ads, etc. have become well-established methods of meeting someone new that would otherwise be impossible.

The downside of focusing on looking for 'The One' is that you can miss meeting some great people and having fun right now. Great nights out with friends, dating aside, can be ruined when your eyes are darting about looking for someone special to meet. Friends can very annoyed because they feel like you're elsewhere – your attention isn't exactly on being sociable with them and just enjoying yourself. And, for you, it becomes piti-ful if heading home without meeting someone means you had a bad night out. A much healthier (and happier) approach is to go out and experience having fun with people you like and be open to meeting new people. Okay, this might lack the intensity or headiness of meeting someone whom you find attractive, but if that is all you are looking for then you might find yourself with fewer friends in the future.

When you do meet someone interesting for the first time, it can be both nerve-racking and exciting. You hope you'll like them and they'll like you. Try to enjoy your first date just for the pleasure of meeting someone new. When the date is over, ask yourself the questions, 'How comfortable was I in their company?', 'How comfortable were they?' and 'Am I confident I would enjoy myself as much again in their company?'

Sometimes you will meet someone and feel attracted to them and they will not feel the same way. It's alright to feel disappointed, yet be realistic – you've got to expect a few knock-backs along the way. If you have experienced rejection in your former relationship you might be quite sensitive to this, but don't let it put you off. Very few first dates will turn into second ones, so enjoy each one as it comes along. Alternatively, your date may be quite taken with you and be interested in meeting you again, but you may not be interested and not know quite how to let them down.

Alan (40): 'I met a girl on a blind date. My friend who set it up said she was attractive and was pretty sure I'd like her. I was just out of a long-term relationship and only looking for fun, nothing serious. She was nice alright, but I wasn't really attracted to her. I didn't know how to say I didn't want to meet her again, so we just said goodbye afterwards and because I didn't know what else to do, I kissed her. She took that to mean I liked her and bombarded me with texts the following day. I knew she was hinting at a second date but really I didn't want that. The texts from her went on for days and I responded to the odd one out of guilt but that only seemed to give her the message that I was interested. Couldn't she tell that I wasn't bothered really? I bumped into her a month later and she lifted me out of it in front of my friends. If only I'd known how to let her down, I could have saved myself a lot of hassle.'

185

Guidelines for Dating

I love the expression 'Be yourself; everyone else is taken.' If you are honest, you are less likely to disappoint someone else or put pressure on yourself to be someone you are not. Naturally, you will want to be seen in a favourable light and may be tempted to embellish the truth about yourself somewhat, perhaps to make yourself appear more interesting, but what's the point? The other person will find out sooner or later if you continue to see them. It's similar to avoiding our shadow side because we end up expending a lot of energy in maintaining a mask, only to have the other person leave us when they eventually find out the truth, which isn't that you're not a suitable person, but that you've betrayed them.

Being open and honest also has the added benefit of making it easier for your date to present their authentic or real self. Honesty helps to build trust and I'd feel confident enough to say it's what we all want in a relationship. We want our partners to be someone in whom we trust. We expect it of others and we should also expect it of ourselves. If honesty wasn't there in your last relationship, dating provides the ideal practice ground. Trust comes from knowing that you will be okay, no matter what happens.

As I mentioned earlier, meeting someone new can bring up all kinds of anxieties: 'Maybe they won't like me' or 'I'm too old/young/small/tall/fat/thin.' Whatever it is you are concerned about, it's perfectly alright to admit to your date that you're nervous. They are likely to be anxious too and admitting it can help break the ice. Could it be that the biggest fear is that you won't be able to handle rejection? One really good tip is to keep that first meeting to an hour, in a public place – meet for coffee and stay away from alcohol for obvious reasons. That way you won't be putting yourself under any pressure or be taking unnecessary risks that you may later regret.

It is better, on the first date, not to talk about prior relationships. On a first meeting, people tend to make judgements about the kind of person you are and if you start talking about your past, your date may think you are stuck back there and not really available in the 'right now'. Remember (even if it is only for that hour) that you are in the present moment and what is past is past.

The first date is about seeing if there is a connection between you. Of course, it would also be lovely if you have things in common. People have a tendency to talk about separation if it has happened to both of them, especially if they are newly separated, but be careful you don't get caught up in this. Unfortunately, if you are still holding on to anger or hurt, it will become evident and may put the other person off. It is better to leave such conversations for a time when things became more serious between you. Try to keep sufficient eye contact without looking too intense, and listen to what the other person has to say as well as speaking yourself.

If you both decide that you'd like to keep seeing each other and arrange another date, this is a good sign that you like each other. Many dating experts will advise you to continue to see lots of people. If that option is open to you, it can certainly work to your advantage in terms of experiencing different situations with different personality types. Putting all your eggs in one basket places undue pressure on yourself and the other person. Remember that dating is supposed to be fun. Just take your time and stay relaxed by enjoying other aspects of your life. The more relaxed you are, the easier it is to fall in love again.

Speaking of which, make sure that you have enough time for the other people in your life and the things that you enjoy doing. You will need this to help you stay relaxed. Although you may find yourself becoming focused on meeting someone new, life is about more than just that. Anyway, even if you are dating someone new and you like being with them, this is no prediction of how things will turn out. So pace yourself by continuing to give attention to other areas of your life.

If you continue to date the same person, be clear about your expectations and what you want. If they're not at the same point, i.e. you want to be casual and they are ready to start a relationship or the other way around, a battle of wills can ensue, where each wants the other to be in the same place as them. This is a waste of time and only perpetuates anxiety, frustration and eventually rejection. It can also give you a bad experience of dating and might put you off meeting someone again.

Learning to let someone down if you feel that you don't want to see them anymore is an important part of relating healthily. A common mistake people make is based on the belief that if they don't get in touch or respond to the other's efforts at communicating with them, that person will somehow get the message that they are no longer interested, as in Alan's case. Unfortunately, this can have the opposite effect, causing the other person to cling on, which can become annoying after a while. As part of honest communication, you have a responsibility to yourself, as well as to the other person, to say, 'I don't believe this is the right fit for me.' You might feel awful doing it at the time, since you don't want to hurt the other person. But, believe me, although it might sting in the short term, in the end you will be glad you did it and they will respect you for your honesty, once they are past the rejection. It allows you both to move on with the minimum of pain.

One of the latter stages of separation is a phase called 'second adolescence' where an individual finds themselves becoming experimental and trying new things. This can be a time of great excitement as they set about re-defining themselves. How they approach dating, if they decide to do so, is all part of this. Some people have a lot of casual sex without wanting much else, or find that they are more focused on companionship than being sexual with someone, until they get to know them better. Either way, please ensure that you are practising safe sex, i.e. using condoms, to prevent you having to deal with a nasty STI. This bears repeating as Irish people are still well behind our European and American counterparts for practising safe sex – be responsible for your sexual health.

A final note on becoming involved with someone new if you have children. Your children are probably your greatest responsibility. Your love for and care of them is vitally important to them when they are experiencing such an upheaval in their lives. Introducing someone new can be threatening for them, even if it is welcomed by you. Keep your dating life separate to your children's lives until such time as you know you are in a serious relationship and they are relatively settled. You may want to spend as much time with your new partner as possible, but you still have routines with your children. You are still a parent with responsibilities and they must be met first. If, in time, you would like to introduce your new partner to your children, take it very slowly and for short periods of time, especially on the first few occasions. Do not expect them to like each other. This is a bonus!

Conclusion

Starting over after separation is a complex and life-changing odyssey for most people who have experienced it. Although there are moments of respite, at some point most of us will have to face the pain that comes with the loss that the ending of a meaningful relationship brings.

The stages along the way will teach you new things about yourself – so much so that, by the time you get to the end of the journey, you might hardly recognise the person you once were. You will have become more aware of your own strength and resilience, as well as your limits, and maybe you'll find that an old dog *can* learn new tricks.

There's no doubt that you will find yourself at sea when it comes to your feelings. This is probably the most common experience of separation, yet these waves of emotion worry people the most, especially when they find themselves close to what they imagine to be insanity at times. They think no one can really understand what it is like for them, not really. And perhaps they are right – separation is such an individual experience and unique to each of us that not even the most experienced professional can assume what's coming next.

Suzy Miller, from the Starting Over Show, an event in the UK that helps people to overcome relationship break-up, says: 'This is a new you being born, and the chick doesn't get out of the egg by flapping its wings. Bashing its beak to smash the shell is what is needed. Use the energy and focus that comes from the emotions you are feeling, and act honourably. Lead by example.'

You may doubt yourself from time to time. Sometimes you may even feel devastated, to the point where you feel you can't go on. Something terrible has happened. But somewhere along the way the realisation will hopefully come that perhaps the worst of the hurt is behind you. You may become aware that at a certain juncture you made a choice or a decision about how the separation will define you: either that it will control you for the rest of your life or will allow you into the driver seat of your own life, with you taking responsibility for what happens next. My wish is for you to live your life without blame or shame. It certainly makes more sense to live for now because the present really is a gift. The past is gone and the future is yet to come.

References and Further Reading

Beattie, Melody (1992), *Codependent No More: How to Stop Controlling Others and to Start Caring for Yourself*, Minnesota, US: Hazelden.

Burrett, Jill (2002), *Parenting After Separation: Making the Most of Family Changes*, Sydney, Australia: Finch Publishing.

Byrne, Rhonda (2006), *The Secret*, London, UK: Simon & Schuster.

Crowe, Michael and Ridley, Jane (2000), *Therapy with Couples – A Behavioural-Systems Approach to Couple Relationship and Sexual Problems*, 2nd edition, Oxford, UK: Blackwell Science.

Field, Lynda (1999), *Creating Self-Esteem: Practical Guide to Realising Your True Worth*, UK, Element Books.

Fisher, Bruce and Alberti, Robert (2006), *Rebuilding – When Your Relationship Ends*, 3rd edition, California, US: Impact Publishers.

Gendlin, Eugene T. (2003), *Focusing – How to Open Up Your Deeper Feelings and Intuition*, London, UK: Rider.

Gomez, Lavinia (1998), *An Introduction to Object Relations*, London, UK: Free Association Books Ltd.

Good, Glynis (2008), *When Parents Split: Support, Information and Encouragement for Teenagers*, Dublin, Ireland: Blackhall Publishing.

Gottman, John and Silver, Nan (2007), *The Seven Principles for Making Marriage Work*, London, UK: Orion Books.

Gray, John (1993), *Men Are from Mars, Women Are from Venus: A Practical Guide to Improving Communication and Getting What You Want in Your Relationships,* London, UK: Thorsons.

Gray, John (1999), *Mars and Venus – 365 Ways to Keep Your Love Alive,* London, UK: Vermilion.

Gurman, Alan and Jacobson, Neil (eds) (2002), *Clinical Handbook of Couple Therapy,* 3rd edition, New York, US: Guildford Press.

Kirk, Mary (1998), *Divorce – Living through the Agony,* Oxford, UK: Lion Hudson.

Kübler-Ross, Elizabeth and Kessler, David (2005), *On Grief and Grieving: Finding the Meaning of Grief through the Five Stages of Loss,* London, UK: Simon & Schuster.

Lewis, Thomas, Amini, Fari and Lannon, Richard (2000), *A General Theory of Love,* London, UK: Random House.

Rich, Phil and Linzer Schwartz, Lita (1999), *The Healing Journey through Divorce: Your Journal of Understanding and Renewal,* Chichester, UK: John Wiley & Sons.

Satir, Virginia (1988), *The New Peoplemaking,* California, US: Science and Behaviour Books.

Sax, Leonard (2005), *Why Gender Matters: What Parents and Teacher Need to Know about the Emerging Science of Sex Differences,* New York, US: Broadway Books.

Solomon, Steven D. and Teagno, Lorie J. (2006), *Intimacy After Infidelity: How to Rebuild and Affair-Proof Your Marriage,* California, US: New Harbinger Publications.

Timonen, Virpi, Doyle, Martha and O'Dwyer, Ciara (2009), 'The Role of Grandparents in Divorced and Separated Families', School of Social Work and Social Policy, Trinity College Dublin.

Viorst, Judith (2002), *Necessary Losses,* 2nd edition, London, UK: Prentice Hall & IBD.

Webb, Dwight (1996), *Divorce and Separation Recovery: Ten Stages of Grieving Relationship Loss and Finding Yourself,* New Hampshire, US: Peter E. Randall.

Useful Organisations

Counselling

Accord, Central Office, Columba Centre, Maynooth, Co. Kildare; 01-5053112; www.accord.ie.

Clanwilliam Institute, 18 Clanwilliam Terrace, Dublin 2; 01-6761363; www.clanwilliam.ie.

Family Therapy Association of Ireland (FTAI), 73 Quinn's Road, Shankill, Co. Dublin; 01-2722105; www.familytherapyireland. com.

Irish Association of Counselling and Psychotherapy (IACP), 21 Dublin Road, Bray, Co. Wicklow; 01-2723427; www.iacp.ie.

Irish Association for Humanistic and Integrative Psychotherapy Ltd (IAHIP), 44 Northumberland Avenue, Dun Laoghaire, Co. Dublin; 01-2841665; www.iahip.org.

Relationships Ireland, 38 Upper Fitzwilliam Street, Dublin 2; 1890-380380; www.relationshipsireland.com.

Domestic Violence

Amen (confidential helpline, a support service and information for male victims of domestic abuse), St Anne's Resource Centre, Railway Street, Navan, Co. Meath, 046-9023718.

COSC, The National Office for the Prevention of Domestic, Sexual and Gender-Based Violence, Department of Justice and Equality, 2nd Floor, Montague Court, Montague Street Dublin 2; 01-4768680; www.cosc.ie.

MOVE Ireland (Men Overcoming Violence), Unit 2, First Floor, Clare Road Business Mall, Clare Road, Ennis, Co. Clare; 065-684 8689; www.moveireland.ie.

SAFE Ireland, 27 Church Street, Athlone, Co. Westmeath; 0906-479078; www.safeireland.ie.

Women's Aid, Everton House, 47 Old Cabra Road, Dublin 7; 1800-341900; www.womensaid.ie.

Solicitors, Collaborative Law, Mediation and Financial

Alternative Dispute Resolution (ADR), www.divorceinireland.net.

Association of Collaborative Practitioners (ACP), www.acp.ie.

Citizens Information Board, Lo-Call: 1890-777121 or 021-4521600; www.citizensinformation.ie.

Family Mediation Ireland, The Calmon Clare Building, Gort Road Business Park, Ennis, Co. Clare; 01-5242217/065-6848624.

Free Legal Advice Centres (FLAC), 13 Lower Dorset Street, Dublin 1; 01-8745690; www.flac.ie.

Legal Aid Board, Quay Street, Cahirciveen, Co. Kerry; 066-9471000; Lo-Call: 1890-615200; www.legalaidboard.ie.

Money Advice and Budgeting Service (MABS), Lo-Call: 1890-283438; www.mabs.ie.

The Family Lawyers Association, www.familylawyers.ie.

The Law Society, Blackhall Place, Dublin 7; 01-6724800; www.lawsociety.ie.

The Mediators' Institute of Ireland, 35 Fitzwilliam Place, Dublin 2; 01-6099190; www.themii.ie.

Children

Barnardos, National Children's Resource Centre, Christchurch Square, Dublin 8; 01-4549699; www.barnardos.ie.

Childline Online, 1800-666666 (freephone); www.childline.ie.

Guardian ad Litem, National Children's Resource Centre, Christchurch Square, Dublin 8; 01-4530355; see the Barnardos website: www.barnardos.ie.

One Family, Cherish House, 2 Lower Pembroke Street, Dublin 2; Lo-Call: 1890-662212 or 01-6629212; www.onefamily.ie.

Parentline, Lo-Call: 1890-927277; www.parentline.ie.

Rainbows Ireland, Loreto Centre, Crumlin Road, Dublin 12; 01-4734175; www.rainbowsireland.com.

Teen Between®, 38 Upper Fitzwilliam Street, Dublin 2; Lo-Call: 1890-380380; www.teenbetween.ie.

Teen Counselling, Mater Dei, Clonliffe Road, Dublin 3; 01-8371892.

Teen-line Ireland, 1800-833634 (freephone); www.teenline.ie.

Treoir, Gandon House, Custom House Square, IFSC, Dublin 1; Lo-Call: 1890-252084; 01-6700120; www.treoir.ie.

Other Useful Services

Aware, 72 Lower Leeson Street, Dublin 2; Lo-Call: 1890-303302; www.aware.ie.

The Family Support Agency, St Stephen's Green House, Earlsfort Terrace, Dublin 2; 01-6114100; www.fsa.ie.

The Samaritans, 1850-609090; www.samaritans.org.

Index